# Calligraphy

### A Practical Handbook for the Beginner
by
Muriel M. Parker

Bonanza Books
New York

This 1982 edition is published by Bonanza Books,
distributed by Crown Publishers, Inc.,
by arrangement with Muriel M. Parker.

Previously published as Formal & Informal Italic Calligraphy

Manufactured in the United States of America

Library of Congress Cataloging in Publication Data
Parker, Muriel M.
    Calligraphy, a practical handbook for the beginner
Reprint. Originally published: Formal & Informal Italic Calligraphy. 1980
        1. Writing, Italic--Handbooks, manuals, etc.
        2. Calligraphy--Handbooks, manuals, etc.
        I. Title.
Z43.P24  1982        745.6'1977        82-4171
ISBN : 0-517-381354                    AACR 2

mlkji

# Dedicated with Many Thanks

To my husband, Edward; & my friends Mark Mitchell, Watchmaker & Scribe; Chris Liswell & "Beanie" Norris & the Mousetrap Craft Shop in Fallston, Md., all of whom played a part in my progression from novice to teacher of Calligraphy....

# Foreword

The trace & copy method used throughout this book is a basic learning tool. The Italic letters have a discipline that is necessary to learn before attempting to create the letters freely, whether in the formal Calligraphic mode ~or~ the informal Cursive mode...

Learning a new discipline, such as Italic, presents difficulties rooted in old established habits, which must be overcome. Handwriting acquired in early school years is so well set in the subconscious that it can never be completely eliminated....

However, by centering down on a new set of rules for writing it is possible to accommodate another form. The more attractive Italic way can replace the original handwriting & at the same time improve one's deep-seated self-image. Learning Italic adds a new dimension to life...

Practice, of course, is absolutely imperative if one is to break old habits & build new & better ones. Developing hand & memory coordination has been the motivating factor in the planning of all of the practice pages in this book so as to assist each person in acquiring facility in writing the elegantly beautiful Italic hand.

# Introduction

✳ The first tool used is one familiar to everyone — a fine felt tip Flair (penmarker).™ This allows the beginner to become easily acquainted with the Italic letters in single line forms without being concerned with how to properly hold or use the Italic fountain pen . . . . . . . . . . . . . . . . . . . .

✳ The next step is to learn how to handle the chisel edge Italic fountain pen — page 18 — so as to create the sensitive thick & thin line of each letter while writing with the pen edge held at a 45° angle. Pages 19, 20 & 21 are practice pages of simple stroke practice & letter specimens showing the thick & thin strokes, using a large pen nib — B4 . . . . . . . . . . . . . .

✳ There are guide line pages (35 to 40 & 55 to 67) for all six Platignum™ pen nibs. Three of the nibs are numbered — beginning with the largest — B4, then B3 & B2. These are for the larger letters. ~ ~ The other three nibs are identified as Broad, Medium, & Fine. These are used to letter formal texts & for correspondence —— . . . . . . . . . . . . . . . . . . . .

✳ In order to create lovely small letters with Broad, Medium & Fine nibs it is important that the beginning student work at first with the larger B4, B3, & B2 nibs for a lengthy period of time. ~ After concentrated practice with larger letters — they become memorized & writing with smaller nibs is an easy adaptation without losing the subtle distinctions & nuances of each letter . . . . . . . . . . . . .

# Distinctive Characteristics of Italic Letters

1. pen edge is held at a <u>45°</u> angle on the paper ~ this <u>never</u> <u>changes</u>

2. the letters are written preferably on a <u>5°</u> slant ( they can be <u>vertical</u> but no more than <u>10°</u> slant

vertical 5° 10°

3. There are letter families & similarities

~ adbgpq    all of these letters have a "pocket" shape in the body of the letter ~

~ bhkmnp    these letters branch <u>over</u> <u>diagonally</u> from the <u>midpoint</u> of the beginning vertical stroke

~ yadgqu    these letters branch <u>under</u> <u>diagonally</u> up from the bottom of the letter to the midpoint of the ending vertical stroke

~ zfscadgqr    these letters have flat tops

~ zyjfsbp    these letters have flat bottoms

ftilj - are vertical line letters with serifs

eos - are elliptical - not round - eos

~ fgjpqy ~ letters with descending strokes below the body of the letters

ksvwxz - letters with diagonal strokes ~ \/

~ bdfhkl    letters with ascending strokes above the body of the letters

~ <u>serifs</u> ~ the turns at the beginnings & endings of each letter ... sharp pointed beginning serifs ʃ - pijtuy    not 111

... narrow turned beginning serifs ʃ    not 111    ... narrow turned ending serifs ʃ    not LLL

mnrvwx    adlhimnux

~ Eleven of the letters have a triangular open area which is shown with a small triangle drawn in the area ~ abd

~ On pages 1, 2, 4 & 7 this area is shown by horizontal line shading ~ abdghmnpqy ~ ghmnpqy

# Formal Mode Contents

# Cursive Mode

## Contents

ascenders

slash – no dots

waist line

base line

descenders

flat – no hooks

★ Getting acquainted with Italic letters → purchase a tracing paper tablet before beginning

1: place a piece of tracing paper over this page

2: then trace the thin letter at the left of group of 2 letters

2 strokes

3: follow the stroke direction lines on the right hand letter

4: a felt tip Flair pen is a good beginning tool

flat

branching over & branching line

the letters shown are written with ① continuous stroke – except for "t, e & x"

2 strokes

or ②

1

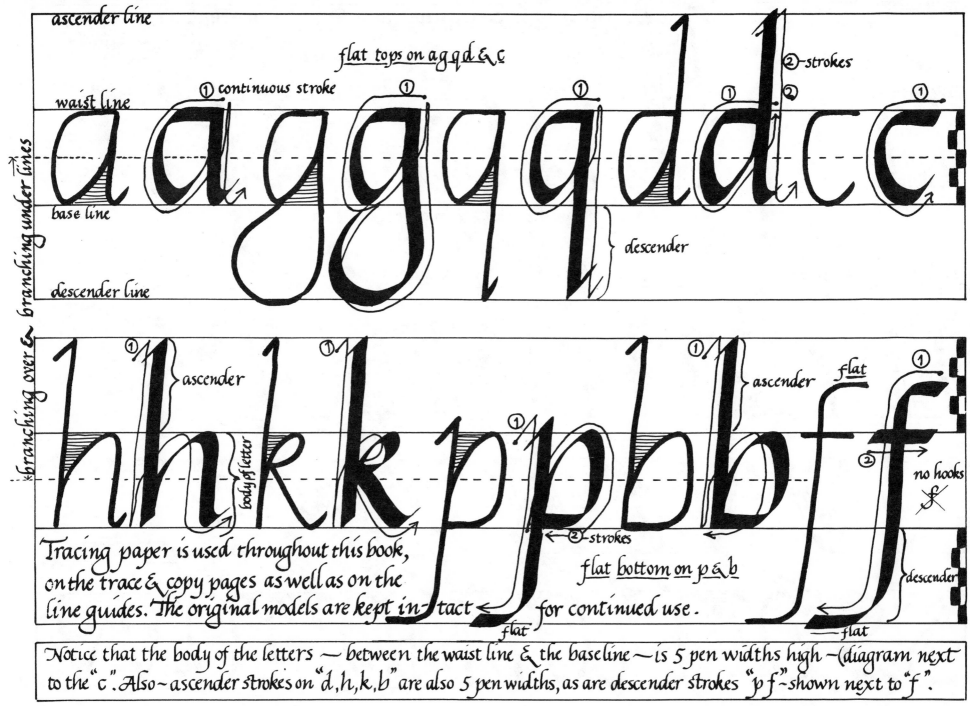

ascender line

flat tops on a g q d & c

waist line

① continuous stroke

branching under lines

base line

descender line

descender

② strokes

descender

branching over &

ascender

body of letter

ascender

flat

no hooks

② strokes

flat bottom on p & b

flat

flat

descender

Tracing paper is used throughout this book, on the trace & copy pages as well as on the line guides. The original models are kept in-tact for continued use.

Notice that the body of the letters — between the waist line & the baseline — is 5 pen widths high ~ (diagram next to the "c". Also ~ ascender strokes on "d,h,k,b" are also 5 pen widths, as are descender strokes "p f"~shown next to "f".

2

ascender line

waist line

branching over & under line – – – – – – – – – – – – – – – – – – – – –

base line

descender line

– – – – – – – – – – – – – – – – – – – – – – – – – – – – – –

(do not write on this page)      Line Guide for Large Letters Practise      (put tracing paper on the page)

3

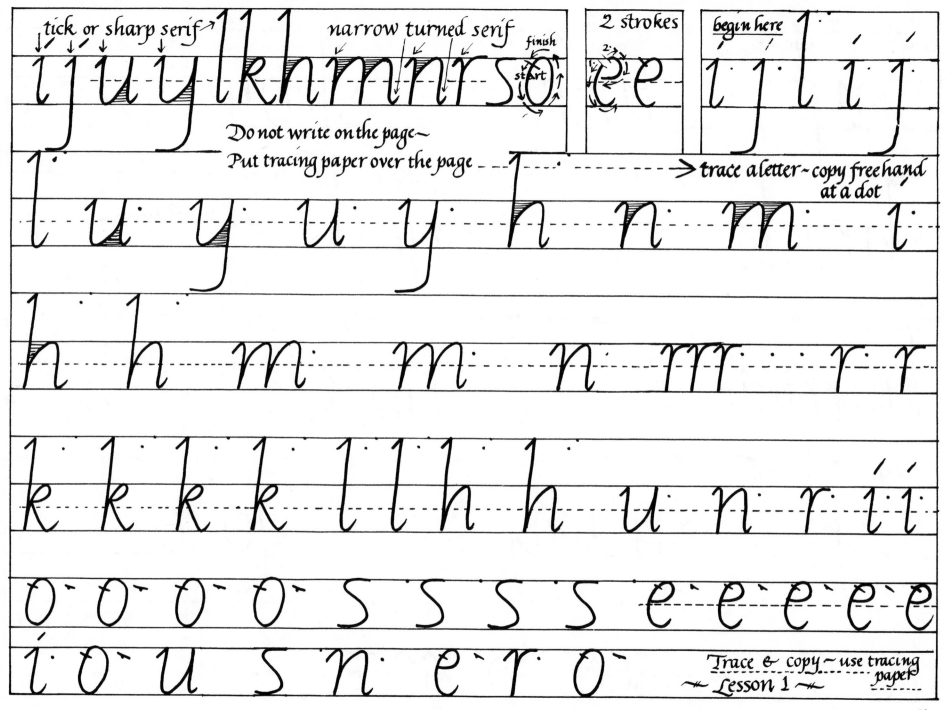

tick or sharp serif      narrow turned serif     finish    2 strokes    begin here

ijuylkhmnrso    ee    ijlij

start

Do not write on the page ~
Put tracing paper over the page ~~~~~~~~~~~~~~~~ → trace a letter ~ copy freehand
at a dot

l u y u y h n m t

h h m m n m r r

k k k k l l h h u n r i i

o o o o s s s s e e e e

i o u s n e r o

Trace & copy ~ use tracing
paper
~ Lesson 1 ~

5

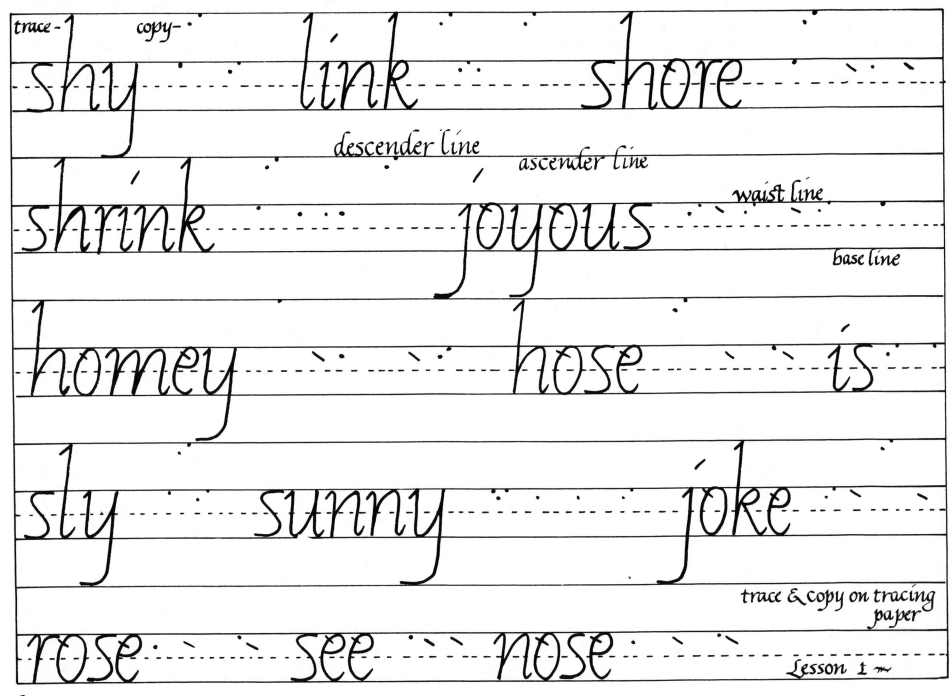

trace-   copy-

shy   link   shore

descender line   ascender line

waist line

shrink   joyous

base line

homey   nose   is

sly   sunny   joke

trace & copy on tracing
paper

rose   see   nose

Lesson 1

6

trace on tracing paper

ornery lonely jury jerky hurry

keep letters close together
copy line

space between words = "o" or "u"

minimum hymn loosen merry

hole    sink    some

trace & copy on tracing paper
Lesson 1

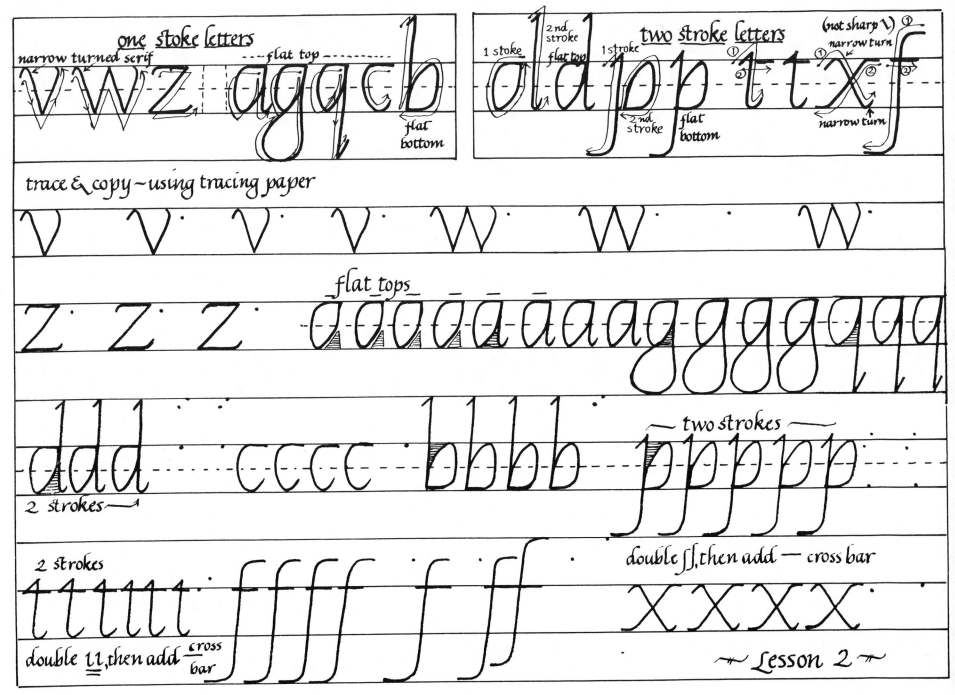

one stoke letters

narrow turned serif ---- flat top ----

two stroke letters

1 stroke  2nd stroke  flat top

(not sharp V)  narrow turn

trace & copy ~ using tracing paper

flat tops

2 strokes

2 strokes

double ∫∫, then add — cross bar

double 11, then add cross bar

~ Lesson 2 ~

8

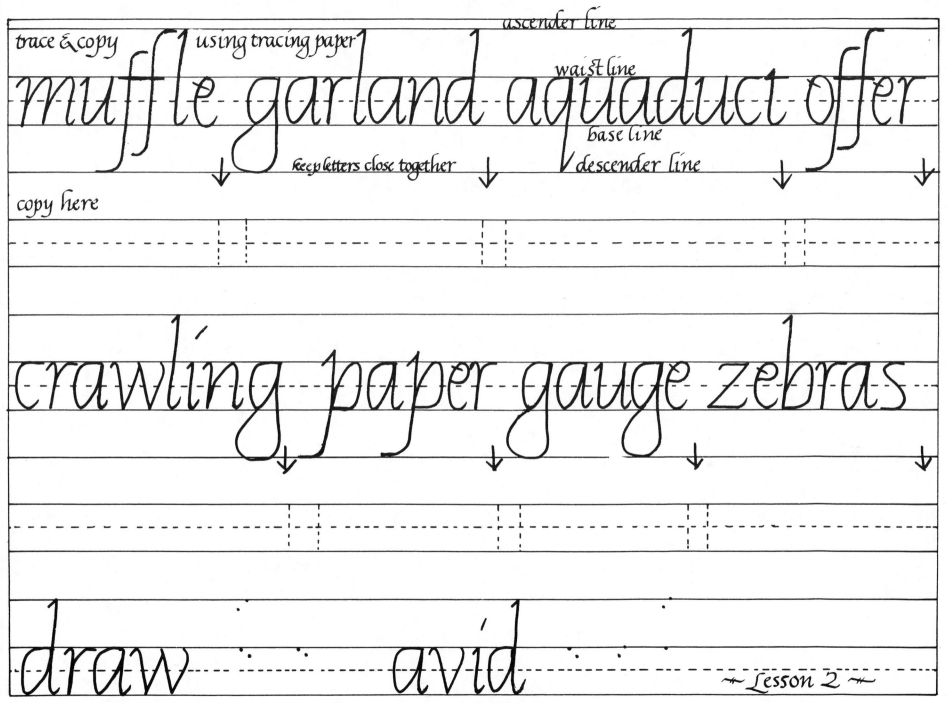

trace & copy · using tracing paper

ascender line

waist line

**muffle garland aquaduct offer**

base line

keep letters close together · descender line

copy here

**crawling paper gauge zebras**

**draw**     **avid**

~ Lesson 2 ~

9

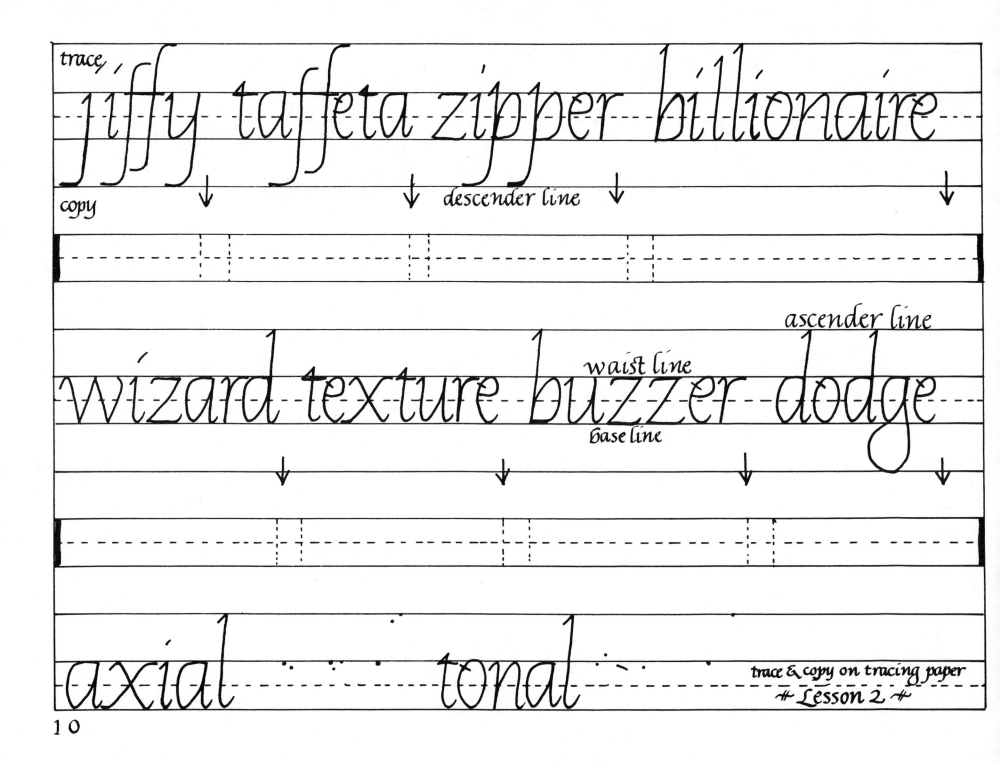

trace

*jiffy taffeta zipper billionaire*

copy

↓       ↓   descender line   ↓         ↓

ascender line

waist line

*wizard texture buzzer dodge*

base line

↓      ↓      ↓      ↓

*axial*       *tonal*

trace & copy on tracing paper

✢ Lesson 2 ✢

ascender line

capital line . . . . . . . . . . . . . . . . . . . . . . . . . . . . . . . . . . . . . . . . . . . . . . . . . . . . . . . . . . . . . . . . . . . . . . . . . . . . . . . . . . . . . . . . 5

waist line

branching over & under line — — — — — — — — — — — — — — — — — — — — — — — — — — — — — — — 5 *pen widths*

base line

— 5

descender line

base line

base line

base line

base line

Body of letter height - 5 pen widths ~ Platignum B-4 pen nib ~ Calligraphic formal mode ~       1 1

hublrnvai

The best slant ranges from vertical to 10°

hublrnvai

hublrvai

Bad slant ranges from 12° to 45°

hublrnva

letters lose Italic beauty ~ are spindly

hublrnva

5°

10°

20°

30°

40°

place your letters over these slanted lines to check for the best slant

12

The Platignum Lettering Fountain Pen Set
consists of a pen barrel &
6 interchangeable nibs
B4 ~ B3 ~ B2 ~ B (Broad) ~ Medium ~ Fine

The Platignum Pen set is a reliable "workhorse" that has a long life when properly cared for as shown on the following pages.

This book was planned for use with the Platignum Fountain Pen Set — 6 pen sizes.

This book can be used with the Osmiroid Lettering set successfully. B4 & B3 nibs are slightly smaller.

The Osmiroid Lettering Set

This book is not designed for use with the →

Sheaffer Cartridge Pen Set

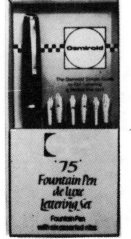

There are the same number of interchangeable nibs in this set as in the one above ~ 6; also labelled B4, B3, B2, Broad, Medium, & Fine. This pen performs satisfactorily. It is more difficult to clean than the one above.

There are only 3 nibs in the Sheaffer Pen Set — Broad, Medium, Fine. These are not the same as Platignum or Osmiroid Broad Medium & Fine nibs.

**NoNonsense pens by SHEAFFER**

13

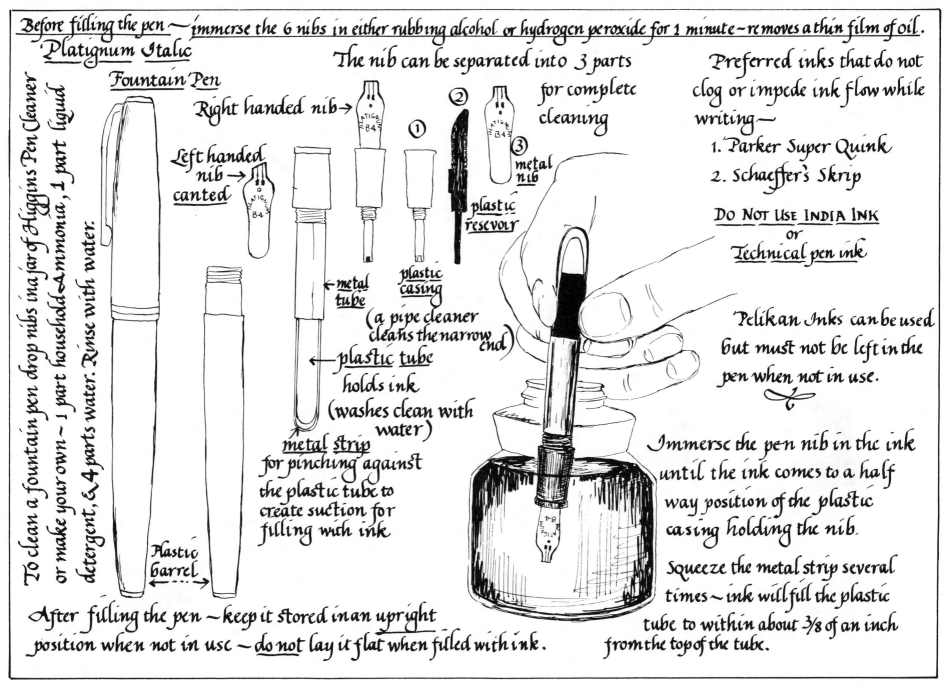

Before filling the pen — immerse the 6 nibs in either rubbing alcohol or hydrogen peroxide for 1 minute — removes a thin film of oil.

'Platignum Italic
Fountain Pen

Right handed nib →

Left handed nib → canted

The nib can be separated into 3 parts for complete cleaning

① ② ③
metal nib

plastic resevoir

metal tube

plastic casing

(a pipe cleaner cleans the narrow end)

← plastic tube holds ink
(washes clean with water)

metal strip for pinching against the plastic tube to create suction for filling with ink

Plastic barrel

To clean a fountain pen drop nibs in a jar of Higgins Pen Cleaner or make your own ~ 1 part household Ammonia, 1 part liquid detergent, & 4 parts water. Rinse with water.

After filling the pen — keep it stored in an upright position when not in use — do not lay it flat when filled with ink.

Preferred inks that do not clog or impede ink flow while writing —
1. Parker Super Quink
2. Schaeffer's Skrip

DO NOT USE INDIA INK
or
Technical pen ink

Pelikan Inks can be used but must not be left in the pen when not in use.

Immerse the pen nib in the ink until the ink comes to a half way position of the plastic casing holding the nib.

Squeeze the metal strip several times ~ ink will fill the plastic tube to within about 3/8 of an inch from the top of the tube.

14

# 3 Steps to prepare a New ~ unused Platignum Lettering Fountain Pen Set for use in writing the Italic Alphabet

1. The 6 nibs marked (& labeled) B4, B3, B2, B or Broad, Medium & Fine, when new, have a thin film of a protective coating on the metal nib ~ which must be removed so as to have the correct flow of the ink.

   ✳ put all six nibs into a small container of either rubbing alcohol or hydrogen peroxide for 1 or 2 minutes ~ then wipe dry on the outside.

2. There is a fine line of distinction between where the parts of each nib assembly are correctly or incorrectly in position for easy writing & steady, even ink flow. ~ A close look at the under side of each nib assembly is necessary to determine whether or not the metal pen edge is down far enough into the white plastic casing. (Some of the plastic casings are black.)

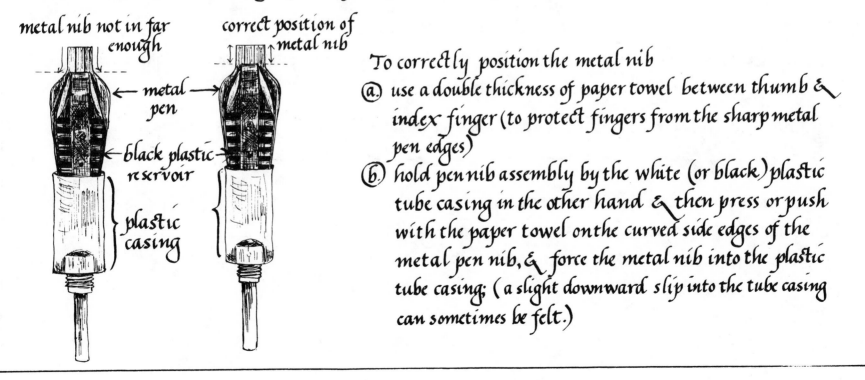

metal nib not in far enough

correct position of metal nib

← metal pen →

black plastic reservoir

plastic casing

To correctly position the metal nib

ⓐ use a double thickness of paper towel between thumb & index finger (to protect fingers from the sharp metal pen edges)

ⓑ hold pen nib assembly by the white (or black) plastic tube casing in the other hand & then press or push with the paper towel on the curved side edges of the metal pen nib, & force the metal nib into the plastic tube casing; (a slight downward slip into the tube casing can sometimes be felt.)

15

3. Often the 2 or 3 sections of the metal nib tips are out of line. (even in a newly purchased set) This must be corrected before the pen will write satisfactorily.

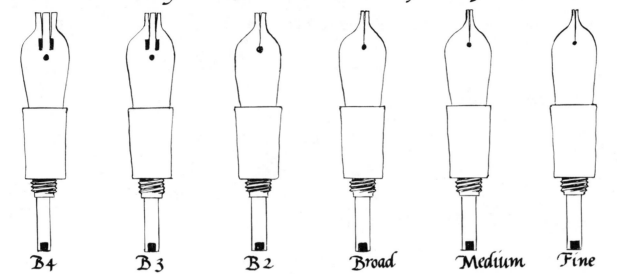

| B 4 | B 3 | B 2 | Broad | Medium | Fine |

Sometimes the slits between the 2 or 3 sections of the pen edge are separated so that light can be seen through them.

Also there are irregularities that may appear on some metal nib EDGES — looking "head on" at the edge

Needle-nose pliers can be used to carefully line up the irregular edges & to press the sides of the nib edges together to produce nib sections that are close together ~ as shown

# How to Make a "Dip" Pen with Platignum
## Fountain Pen Metal Nibs

Each of the Platignum Fountain Pen nibs, (B-4, B-3, B-2, Broad, Medium & Fine) when separated from the nib assembly, can be made into a so-called "dip pen" & can be used to write or letter with all of the thicker inks ~ such as India inks, Sumi liquid or stick inks & mechanical pen inks such as FW & Mars.

① A pen holder

No 130   KOH-I-NOOR
Germany

&

② A William Mitchell slippon reservoir ~ can be made to fit the Platignum Fountain pen nibs with needle nose pliers.

Top

under side of reservoir      Bottom

a- The slippon reservoirs are manufactured to fit Mitchell round hand pen nibs ~ ~ but

b- With needle nose pliers the slippon reservoirs can be curved to fit the Platignum Fountain pen nibs

from this → ⌣ to this → ⌄
(looking at the bottom edge)

c- The slippon reservoir must be adjusted by bending the tapered rounded top slightly forward so that it will touch the under side of the nib ~ thus able to hold ink under the nib.

under side of pen nib

from this → to this →
(side view)

d- the reservoir is now able to be slipped on to any of the 6 Platignum Fountain Pen nibs from the bottom of each nib.

SLIPPON RESERVOIR
WILLIAM MITCHELL'S NO. 2
top side of reservoir

reservoir                side view

pen nib

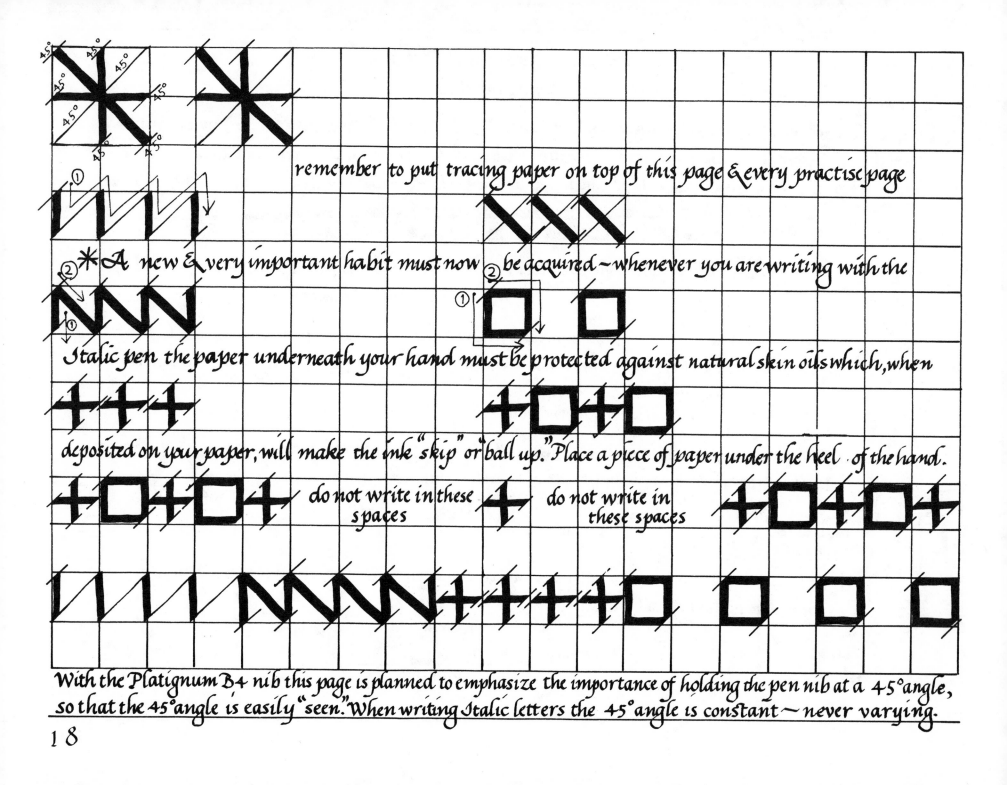

remember to put tracing paper on top of this page & every practise page

✳ A new & very important habit must now be acquired ~ whenever you are writing with the

Italic pen the paper underneath your hand must be protected against natural skin oils which, when

deposited on your paper, will make the ink "skip" or "ball up." Place a piece of paper under the heel of the hand.

do not write in these
spaces

do not write in
these spaces

With the Platignum B4 nib this page is planned to emphasize the importance of holding the pen nib at a 45°angle,
so that the 45°angle is easily "seen." When writing Italic letters the 45°angle is constant ~ never varying.

18

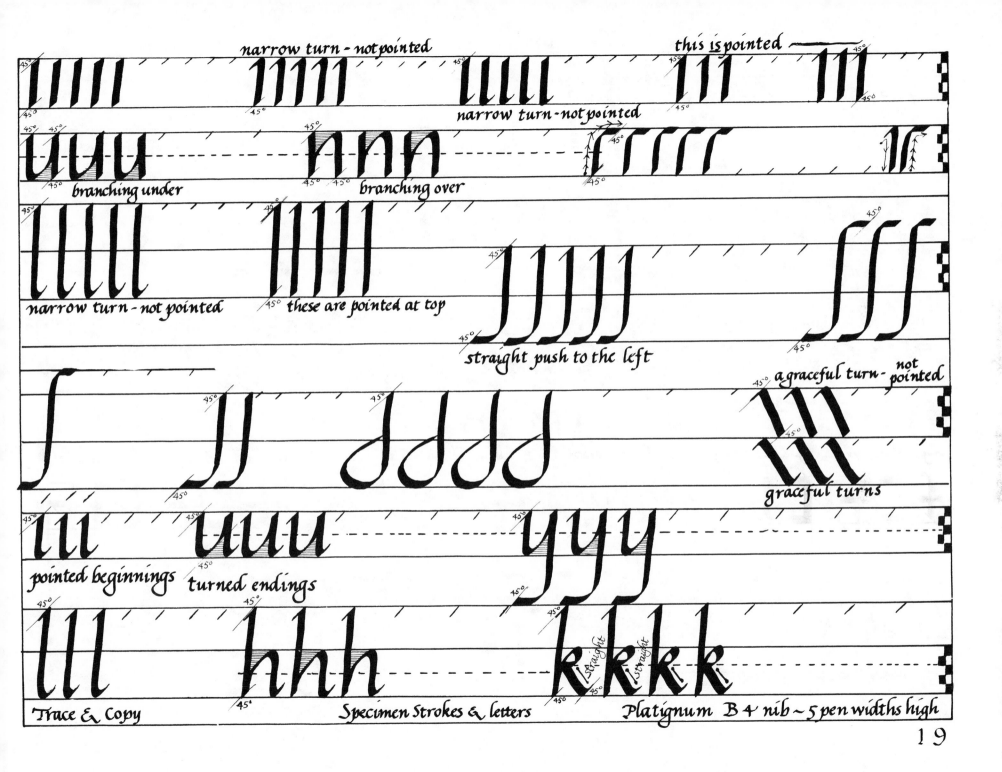

narrow turn - not pointed

this is pointed

narrow turn - not pointed

branching under

branching over

narrow turn - not pointed

these are pointed at top

straight push to the left

a graceful turn - not pointed

graceful turns

pointed beginnings

turned endings

straight

straight

Trace & Copy

Specimen Strokes & letters

Platignum B 4 nib ~ 5 pen widths high

19

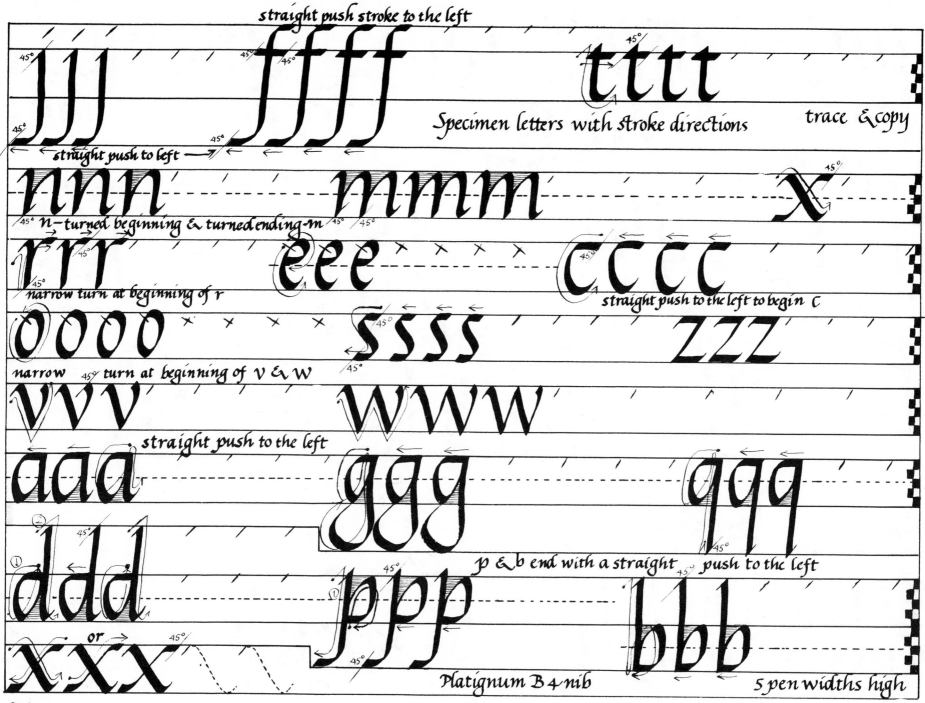

straight push stroke to the left

jjj ffff tttt

Specimen letters with stroke directions     trace & copy

straight push to left

nnn mmm x

45° n – turned beginning & turned ending - m

rrr eee cccc

narrow turn at beginning of r          straight push to the left to begin c

oooo ssss zzz

narrow    45° turn at beginning of v & w

vvv www

straight push to the left

aaa ggg qqq

p & b end with a straight    push to the left

ddd ppp

or

xxx bbb

Platignum B4 nib          5 pen widths high

20

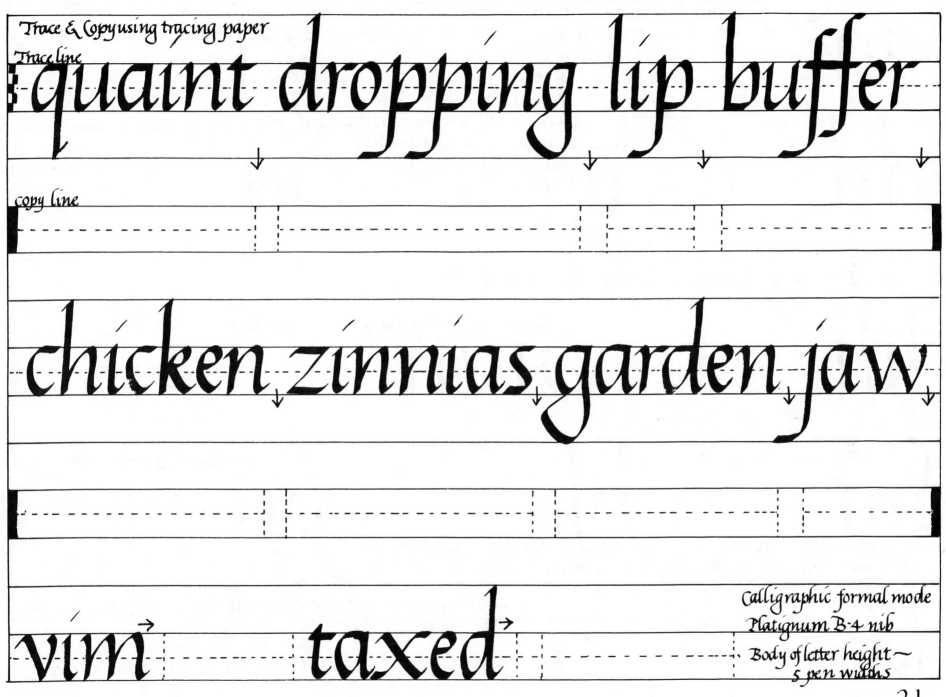

Trace & Copy using tracing paper

Trace line

quaint dropping lip buffer

copy line

chicken zinnias garden jaw

vim    taxed

Calligraphic formal mode
Platignum B·4 nib

Body of letter height ~
5 pen widths

21

Letters that branch under ~ a, u, y, d, g, q

aa    uu    yy

Trace & Copy ~ using tracing paper    These are the letters that
branch under from the base line
& branch over up to the waist line. ~

dd    gg    qq

Letters that branch over ~ h, m, n, b, p, k, & r

narrow turn at beginning & end of m & n

hh    mm

b & p end with a <u>flat</u> push stroke ~ left

nn    bb    pp

All of the letters above have a △ ▽ triangular open area which begins
at the half way point in the body of the letters, ~ characteristic of Italic.

k & r ~ also branch over but above the half way point of the letter body.
narrow turn at beginning of r ~ not pointed

kk    rr    Platignum B-4 nib
Body height of letters ~ 5 pen widths

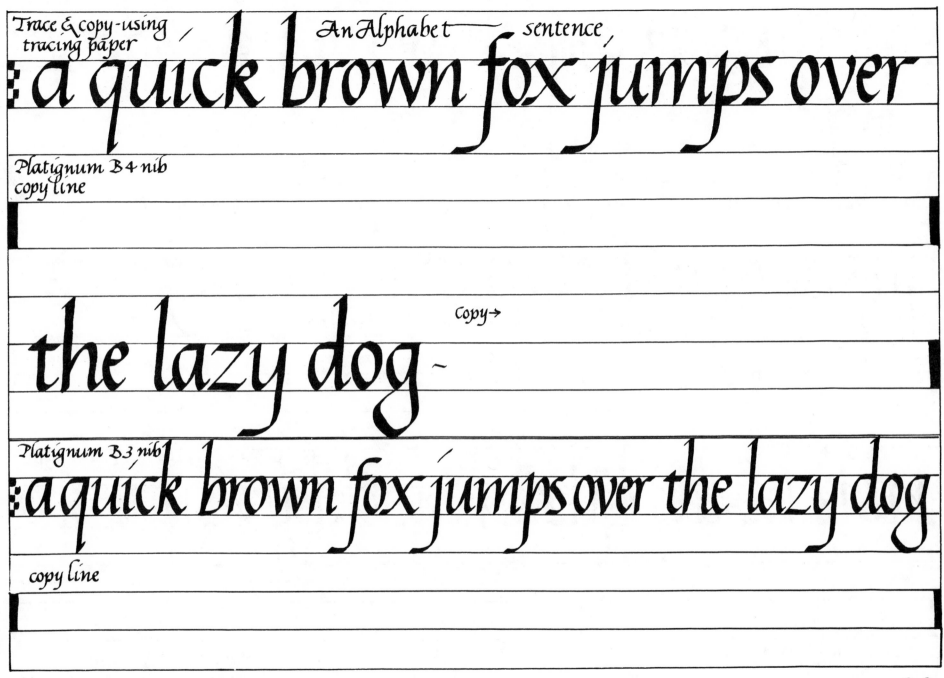

Trace & copy-using
tracing paper

An Alphabet ——— sentence,

a quick brown fox jumps over

Platignum B4 nib
copy line

Copy →

the lazy dog ~

Platignum B3 nib

a quick brown fox jumps over the lazy dog

copy line

Trace

back inside myself within windows

Copy

Use tracing paper for tracing & Copying

Calligraphic formal mode~keep letters close together

jaunty fox foolish making zippered

able history jazzy quickly visual too

5½ pen widths for the body of
the letters

Platignum B-3 nib

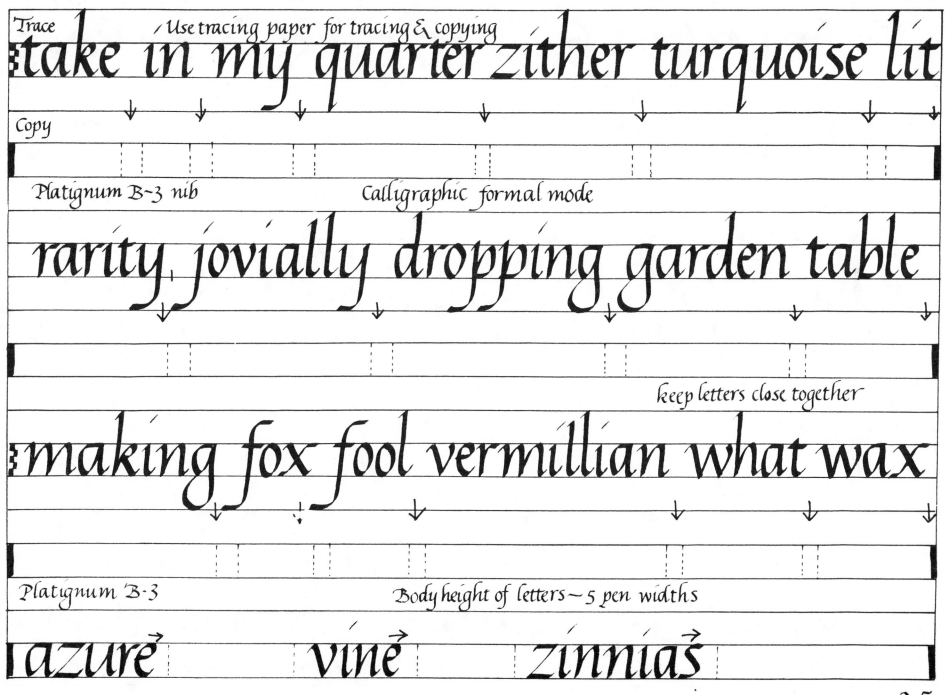

Trace /Use tracing paper for tracing & copying

# take in my quarter zither turquoise lit

Copy

Platignum B-3 nib        Calligraphic formal mode

# rarity jovially dropping garden table

keep letters close together

# making fox fool vermillian what wax

Platignum B-3        Body height of letters ~ 5 pen widths

# azure vine zinnias

25

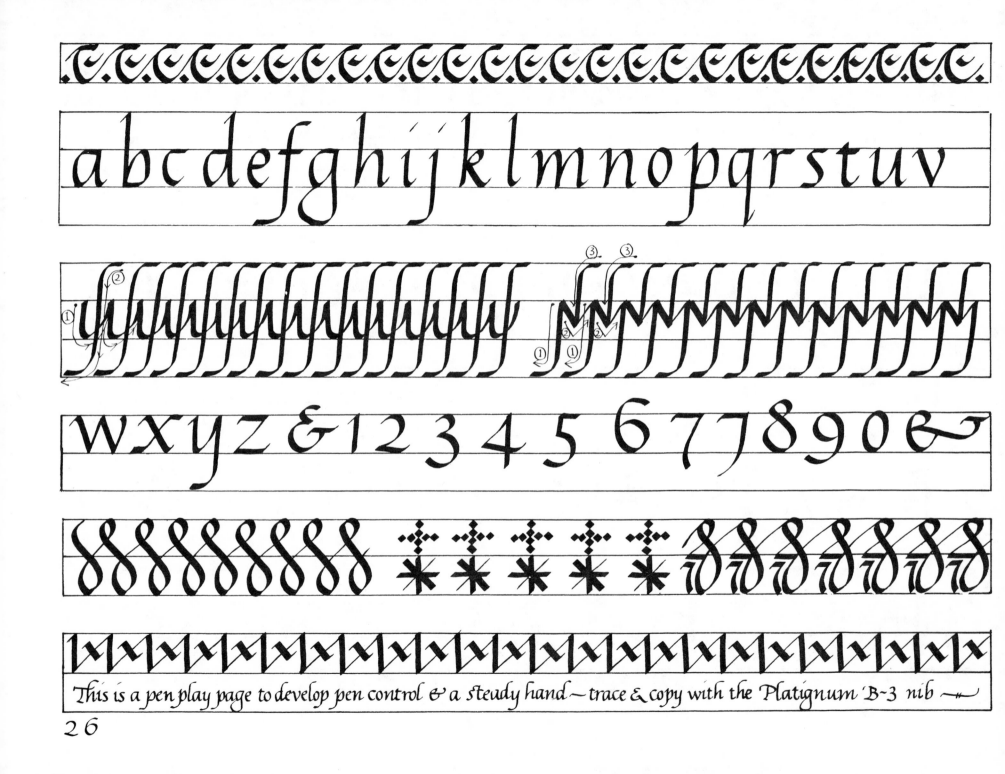

abcdefghijklmnopqrstuv

wxyz & 1234567890

*This is a pen play page to develop pen control & a steady hand — trace & copy with the Platignum B-3 nib*

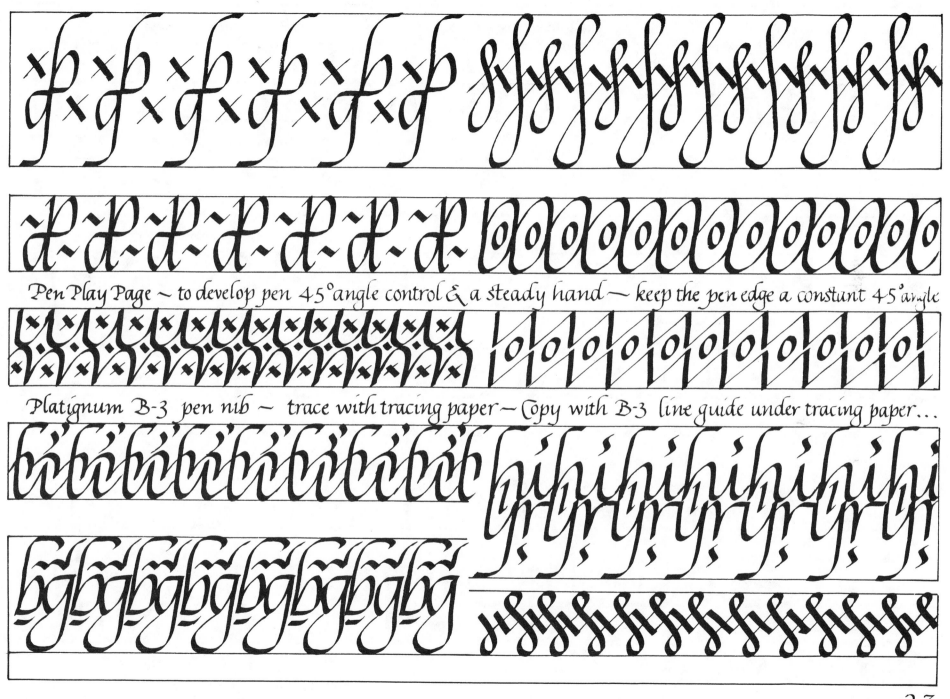

Pen Play Page ~ to develop pen 45°angle control & a steady hand ~ keep the pen edge a constant 45°angle

Platignum B-3 pen nib ~ trace with tracing paper ~ Copy with B-3 line guide under tracing paper...

27

club serifs   Variations of tops of ascenders   "tick" or pointed serifs

bd h k l   bd h k l   hd h k l   bd k h l

Platignum B 3 pen nib

Numbers are generously spaced in a sequence ~ 1 9 8 1   not 1981

Old Style numbers           Modern numbers

1 2 3 4 5 6 7 8 9 0   1 2 3 4 5 6 7 8 9 0

& & & & & & & ~ : ; , ! ? ~ " " ( )

Ampersand ~ Latin ET = and ~ used often instead of the word "and" in Italic.   Punctuation marks ~

Here are some interesting letter joinings
This "or" shape is from Uncial letters ~ (400 - 600 A.D.)

Variations on letter "q"

st ct sp or pr br are gr ~ q q q q q q

used only with closed letters

Platignum B 3 pen nib         Calligraphic formal mode

28

abcdefghijklmnopqrstuvwxyz

This is the correct 45° angle ◻ in this line of letters.

1.

abcdefghijklmnopqrstuvwxyz

These letters are incorrect. The pen was at too steep an angle ▯ close to 60°.

2.

If your letters need correcting — compare them with lines 2 & 4 to see which incorrect pen angle is your problem.

abcdefghijklmnopqrstuvwxyz

This is the correct 45° angle ◻ in this line of letters.

3.

abcdefghijklmnopqrstuvwxyz

These letters are incorrect. The pen angle was too flat ▭ close to the horizontal

4.

Common errors in letter shapes when the pen edge is not held at a 45° angle on the writing surface.

Platignum B3 nib

| 45° | | | 45° | | | 45° | | | 45° | | | 45° | | |
|---|---|---|---|---|---|---|---|---|---|---|---|---|---|---|
| i | i | i | n | n | n | u | u | u | a | a | a | r | r | r |
| correct | too steep | too flat | correct | too steep | too flat | correct | too steep | too flat | correct | too steep | too flat | correct | too steep | too flat |

29

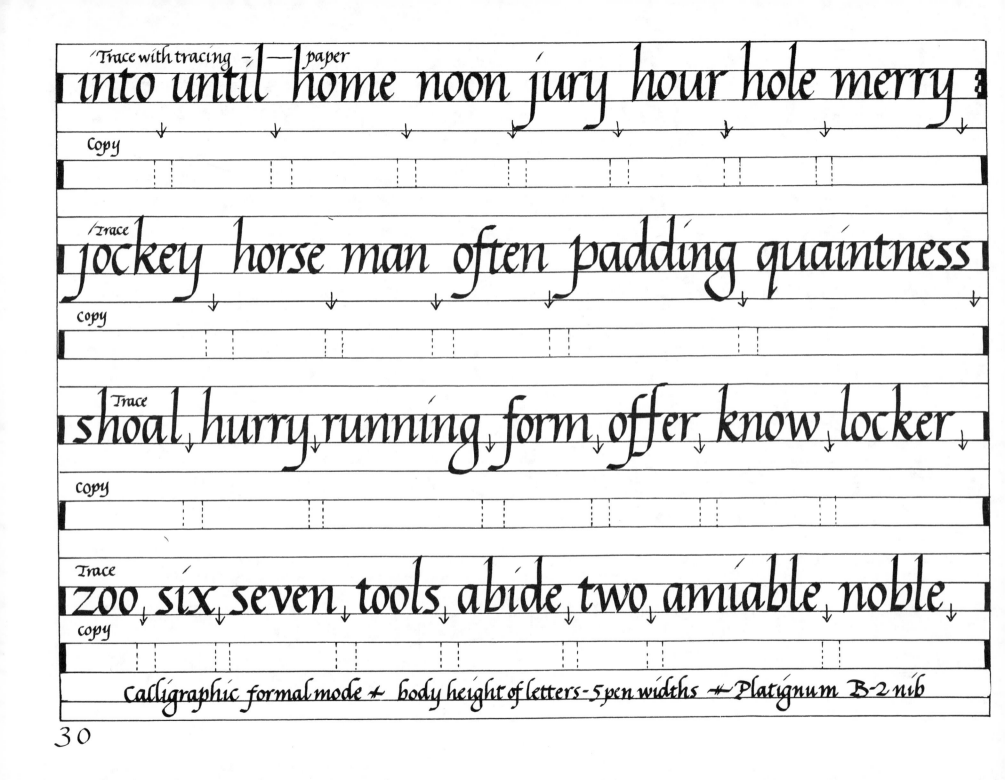

Trace with tracing —|——|paper

into until home noon jury hour hole merry

Copy

Trace

jockey horse man often padding quaintness

Copy

Trace

shoal hurry running form offer know locker

Copy

Trace

zoo six seven tools abide two amiable noble

copy

calligraphic formal mode ✦ body height of letters-5 pen widths ✦ Platignum B-2 nib

Trace

a quick brown fox jumps over the lazy dog

copy

Remember~ the slant of Italic letters is 5° from the vertical

Trace

a quick brown fox jumps over the lazy dog    Platignum Broad nib
(B - nib)

copy

Spaces between words are the width of another letter such as "o e a".

Trace

a quick brown fox jumps over the lazy dog    Platignum Medium nib

copy

In the Calligraphic formal mode the letters of words "love each other" ~ are close together

Trace

a quick brown fox jumps over the lazy dog    Platignum Fine nib

copy

Calligraphic Formal mode

As the pen gets smaller~ the letters also become smaller ~~ BUT ~~ the pen width height is always $\frac{5}{2}$ pen widths

31

O · Q · C · G · D are constructed in a square to emphasize that they are the wide round letters.

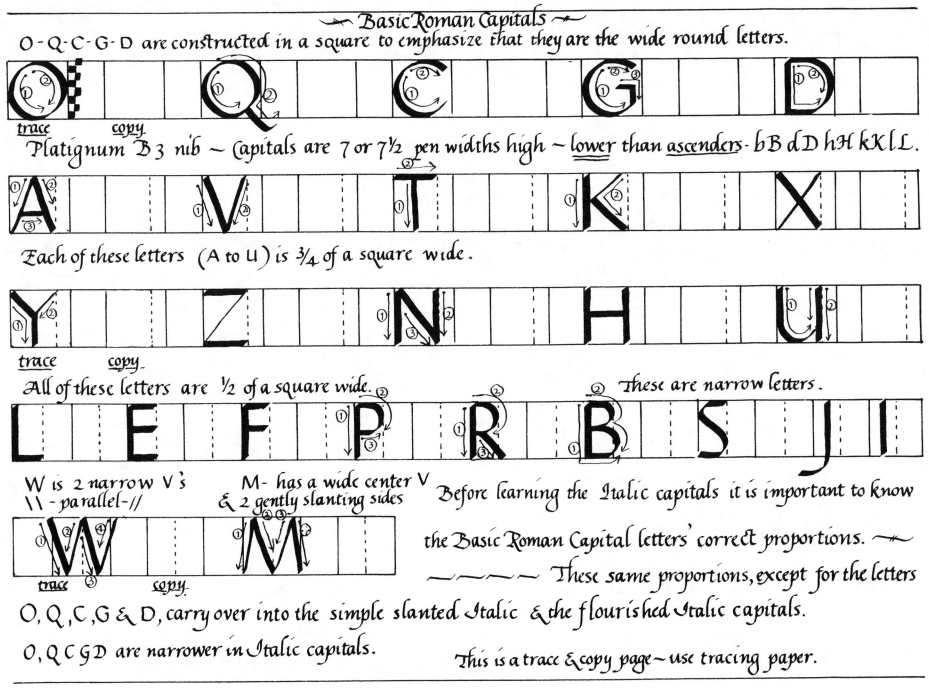

trace    copy

Platignum B 3 nib ~ Capitals are 7 or 7½ pen widths high ~ lower than ascenders · bB dD hH kK lL.

Each of these letters (A to U) is ¾ of a square wide.

trace    copy

All of these letters are ½ of a square wide.    These are narrow letters.

W is 2 narrow V's    M - has a wide center V
\\ - parallel - //    & 2 gently slanting sides

Before learning the Italic capitals it is important to know

the Basic Roman Capital letters' correct proportions. ~

~~~~~ These same proportions, except for the letters

trace    copy

O, Q, C, G & D, carry over into the simple slanted Italic & the flourished Italic capitals.

O, Q C G D are narrower in Italic capitals.

This is a trace & copy page ~ use tracing paper.

Trace — ascenders line — Capital line

a A b B c C d D e E f F g G h H i I

copy

Trace — ascenders line — Capital line

j J k K l L m M n N o O p P q Q

copy

Trace — ascenders line — Capital line

r R s S t T u U v V w W x X y Y z Z

copy — Capitals are 7 or 7½ pen widths high. — Platignum B 3 nib

no serifs — Slanted Simple Roman Capitals — no flourishes

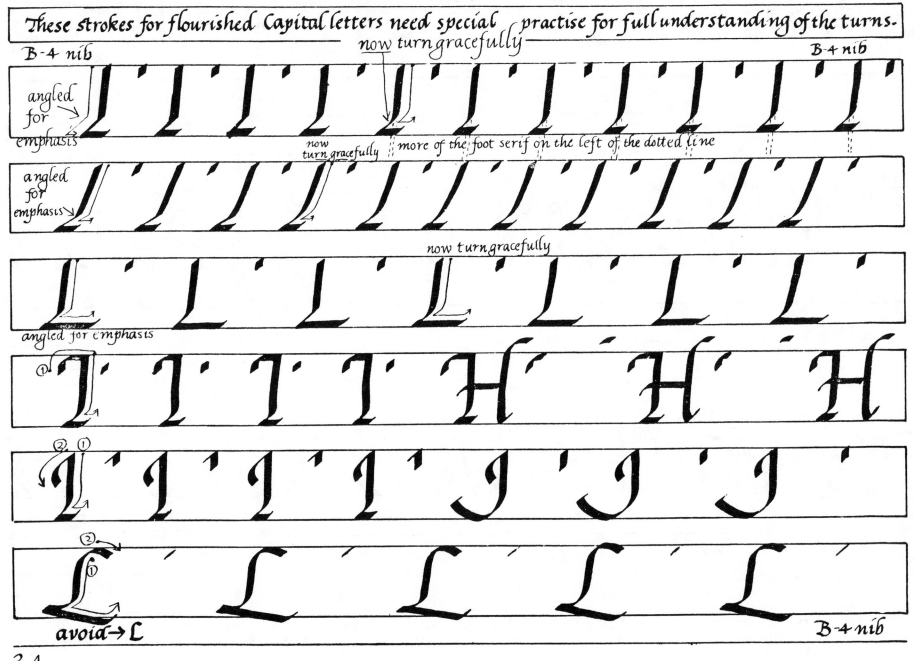

now turn gracefully

B-4 nib

B-4 nib

angled for emphasis

now turn gracefully — more of the foot serif on the left of the dotted line

angled for emphasis

now turn gracefully

angled for emphasis

avoid → L

B-4 nib

34

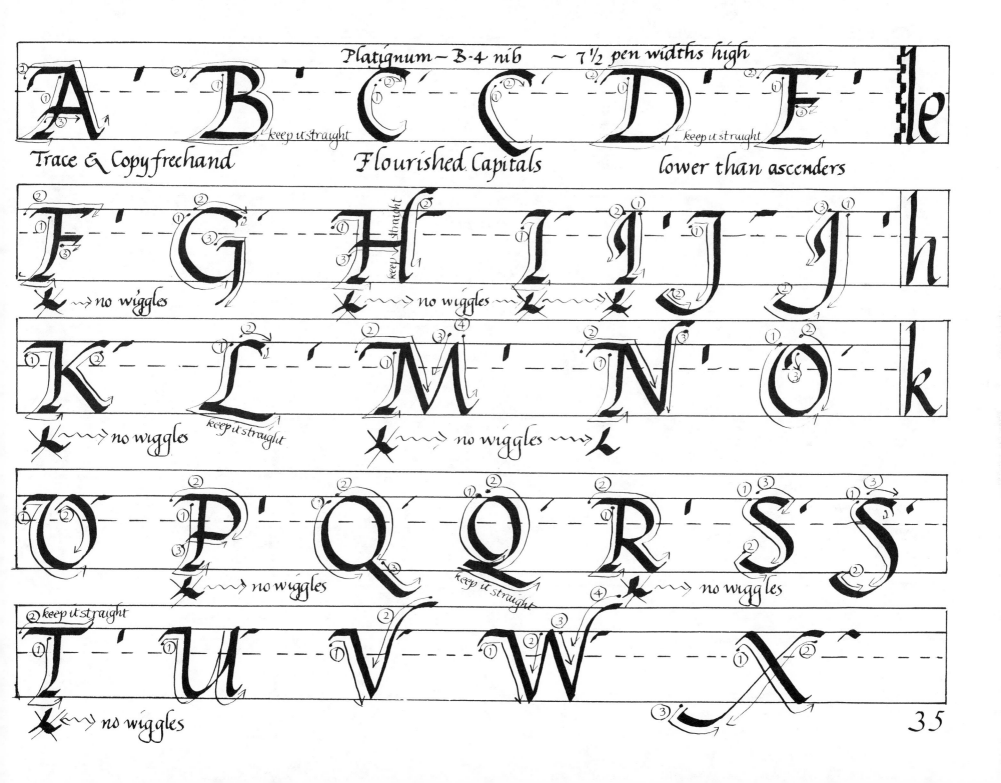

Platignum ~ B-4 nib   ~ 7½ pen widths high

A B C C D D E le

keep it straight     keep it straight

Trace & Copy freehand          Flourished Capitals          lower than ascenders

F G H I I J j h

keep it straight

no wiggles          no wiggles

K L M N O k

no wiggles          keep it straight          no wiggles

U P Q R S S

no wiggles          keep it straight          no wiggles

keep it straight

T U V W X

no wiggles

35

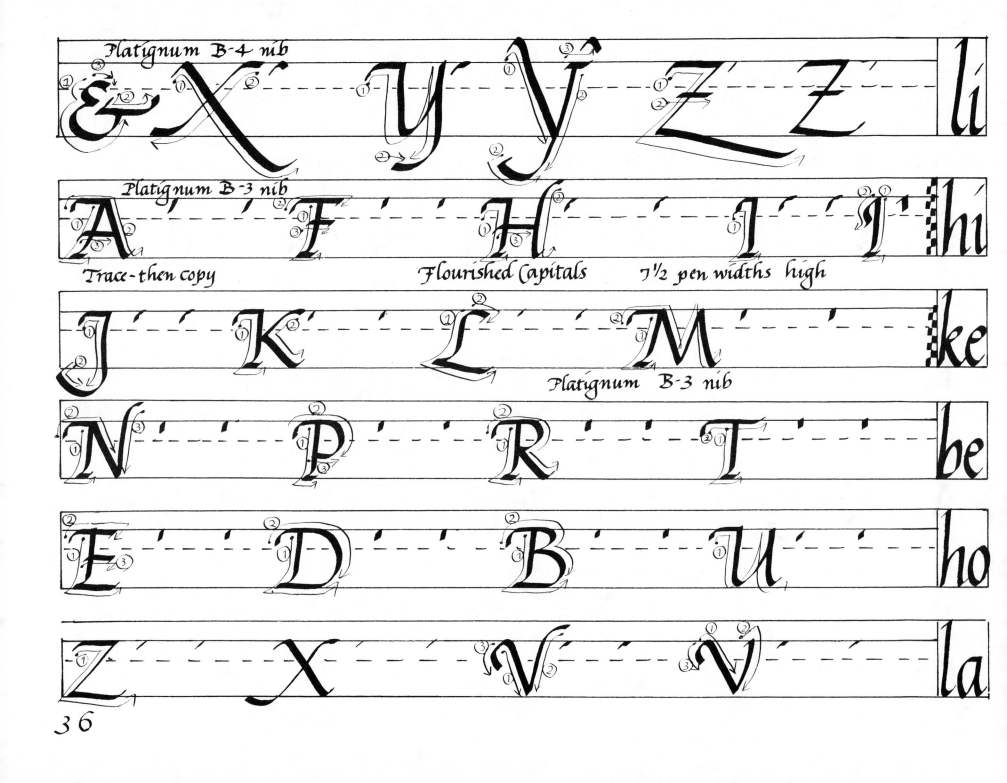

Platignum B-4 nib

& X y Y Z Z    li

Platignum B-3 nib

A F H I I    hi

Trace - then copy    Flourished Capitals    7½ pen widths high

J K L M    ke

Platignum B-3 nib

N P R T    be

E D B U    ho

Z X V V    la

Platignum B-3 nib

7½ pen widths high    Flourished Capitals ~ lower than ascenders

Platignum B-2 nib

ABCDEFGHIJKLMNOPQQ | le

RSTUVWXXYYZZ bbbb & et et

abbcddefffghhijkklllmnopgrstuvwxyyz

37

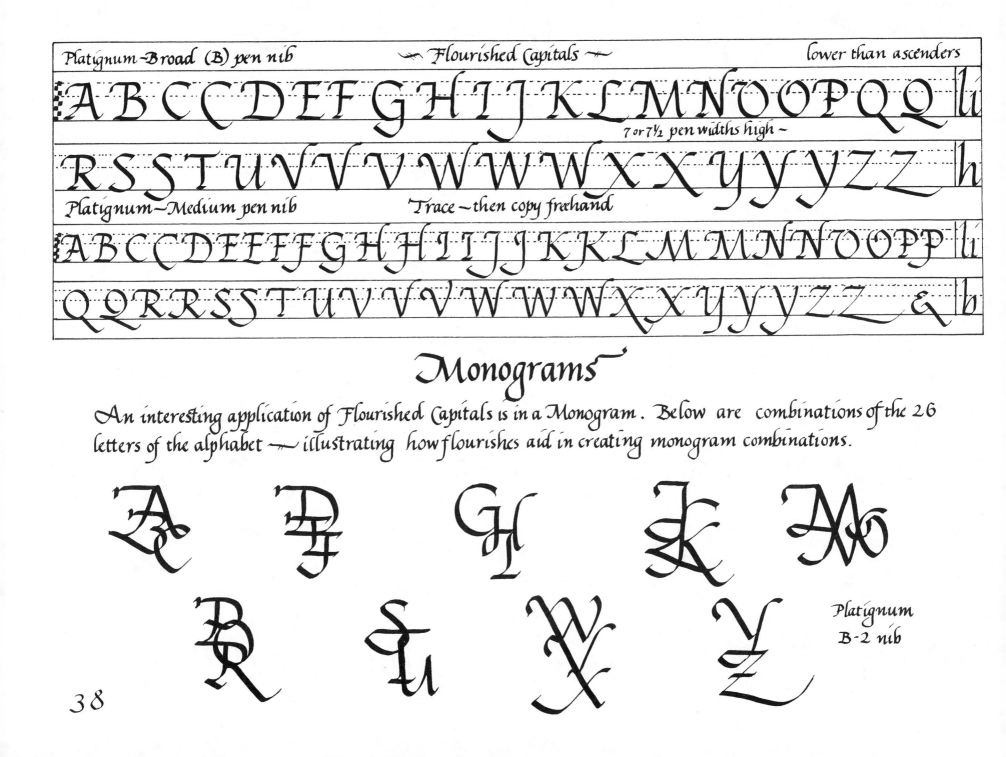

ABCCDEFGHIJKLMN OOPQQ li

7 or 7½ pen widths high ~

RSSTUVVVWWXXYYYZZ h

Platignum—Medium pen nib     Trace—then copy freehand

ABCCDEEFFGHHIIJJKKLMMNNOOPP li

QQRRSSTUVVVWWWXXYYYZZ & b

## Monograms

An interesting application of Flourished Capitals is in a Monogram. Below are combinations of the 26 letters of the alphabet — illustrating how flourishes aid in creating monogram combinations.

Platignum
B-2 nib

38

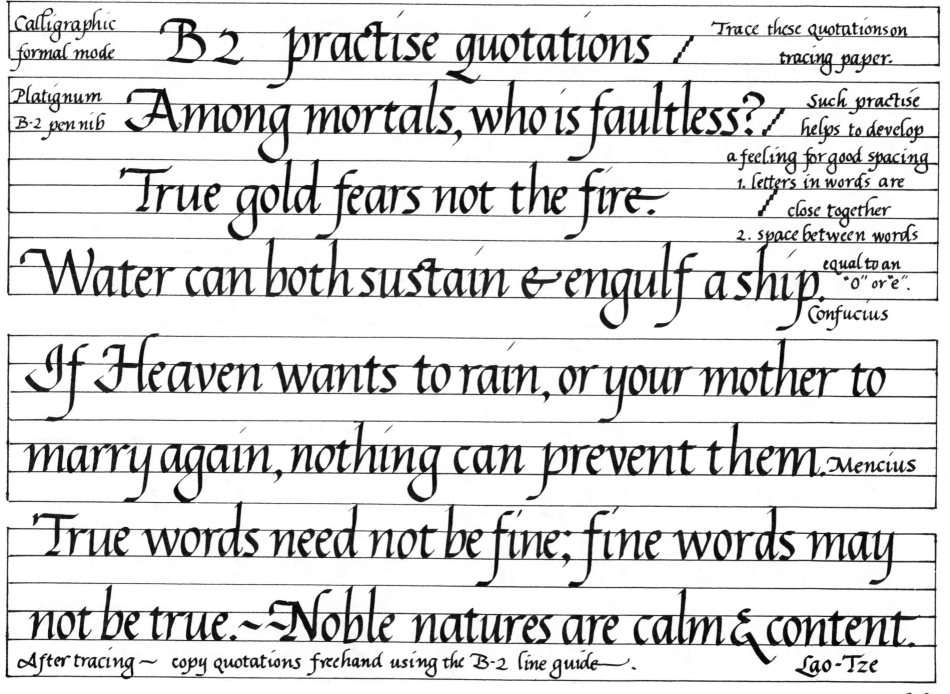

B2 practise quotations

Trace these quotations on tracing paper.

Platignum B-2 pen nib

Among mortals, who is faultless?

Such practise helps to develop a feeling for good spacing

True gold fears not the fire.

1. letters in words are close together
2. space between words equal to an "o" or "e".

Water can both sustain & engulf a ship.

Confucius

If Heaven wants to rain, or your mother to

marry again, nothing can prevent them. Mencius

True words need not be fine; fine words may

not be true.~Noble natures are calm & content.

After tracing~ copy quotations freehand using the B-2 line guide~.

Lao-Tze

39

Better not to do kindnesses at all than to do them in the hope of recompense.

What is whispered in the ear is heard miles away.

Think twice & say nothing...                    Lao-Tse

If so designed, you will meet each other; if not, you will miss each other. Lao Tse

Birth is not a beginning: death is not an end.

Act with kindness, but do not exact gratitude...

A lost inch of gold may be found; a lost inch of time ~ never...                    Confucius

Yellow gold has its price; learning is priceless...

Extensive reading is a priceless treasure....                    Mencius

40

God respects me when I work, but He loves me when I sing...

The smile that you send out returns to you. ∕ ~ Tagore

Only the ignorant man becomes angry. The wise man understands. Indian Wisdom

Even the severed branch grows again, & the sunken moon returns:

a wise person who ponders this is not troubled in adversity. Bhartrhari

What you send into the lives of others comes back into your own...

One joy dispels a hundred cares. Oriental Wisdom

Good words are like a string of pearls. Noble natures are calm & content. Lao-Tse

Whence did the wondrous art arise of painting speech, & speaking to the eyes?

That by tracing magic lines are taught how to embody & how to color thought.
William Massey

Have you had a kindness shown? Pass it on; 'Twas not given for thee alone, pass it on.
Henry Burton

41

Trace & Copy exercise ~ for the Fine pen nib ~ in the Formal Calligraphic & Informal Cursive Modes

Calligraphy may be considered as including formal & informal handwriting. There is a clearly marked division between formal Calligraphic & informal cursive ~ formal Calligraphic being distinctly separate letters ~ while informal cursive letters are joined with certain well defined joins or "ligatures"......

The tool used to create these lovely letters is a straight edged pen, which when held at a 45° angle makes thick & thin strokes with a natural pressure that is even & light......

Italic Calligraphy may be described as a skill in which an understanding of the manipulation of the straight or chisel edged pen is paramount; ~ the edge of the pen does not vary from 45° as one is writing ~ either formal Calligraphic mode or informal Cursive mode......

Cursive informal Italic handwriting is for writing letters of correspondence. With much practise & determination/effort cursive Italic can be written with considerable speed......

Formal Italic, calligraphic mode, on the other hand, is more carefully written, slowly & with complete planning before beginning to write on a fine piece of paper......

42

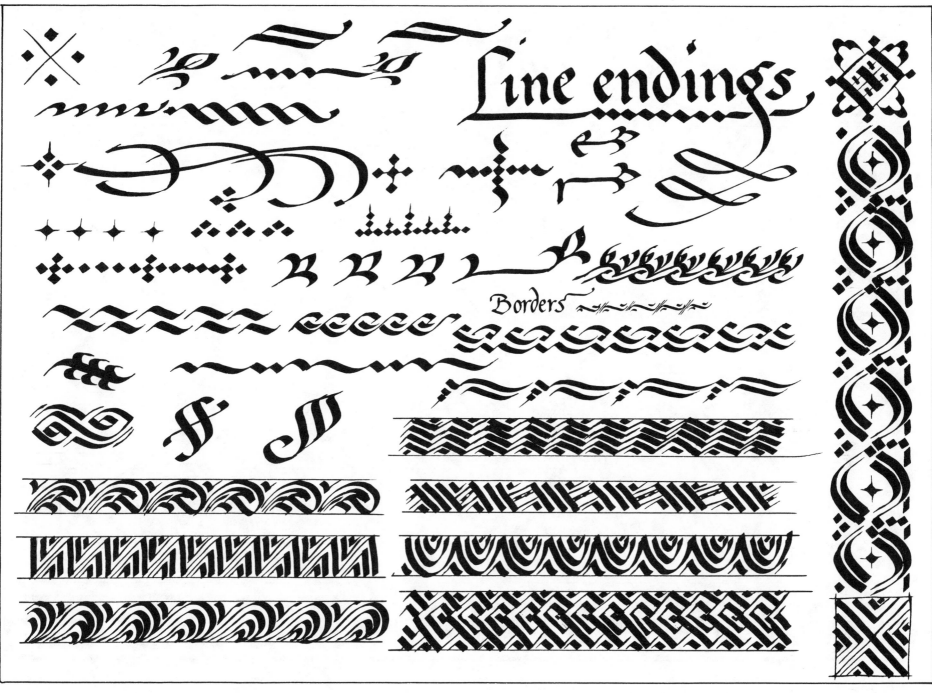

Line endings

Borders

43

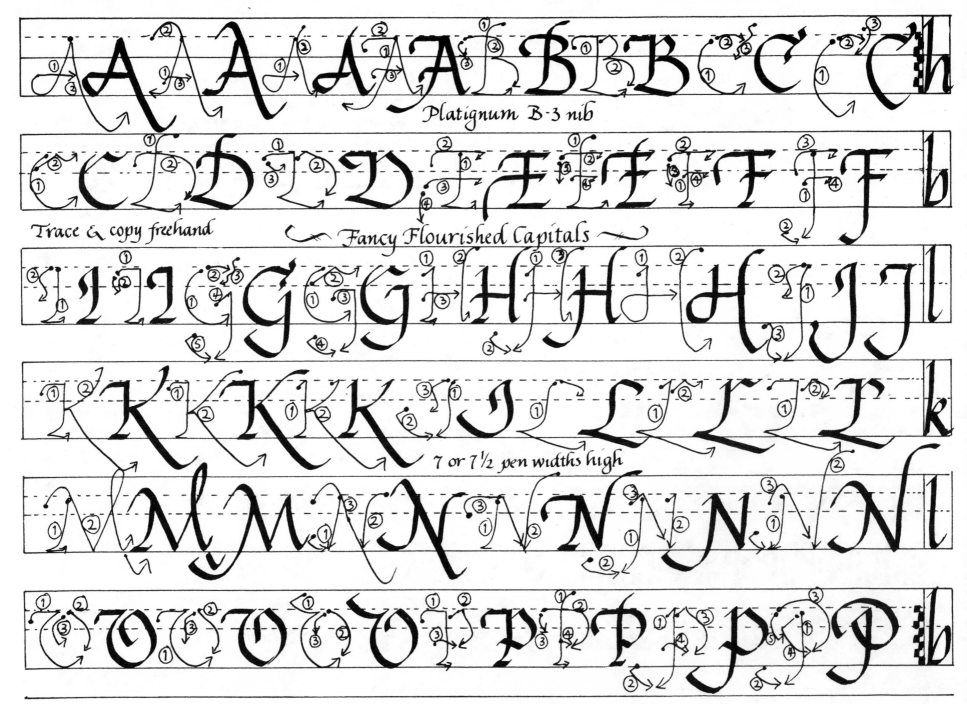

Platignum B-3 nib

Trace & copy freehand

Fancy Flourished Capitals

7 or 7½ pen widths high

44

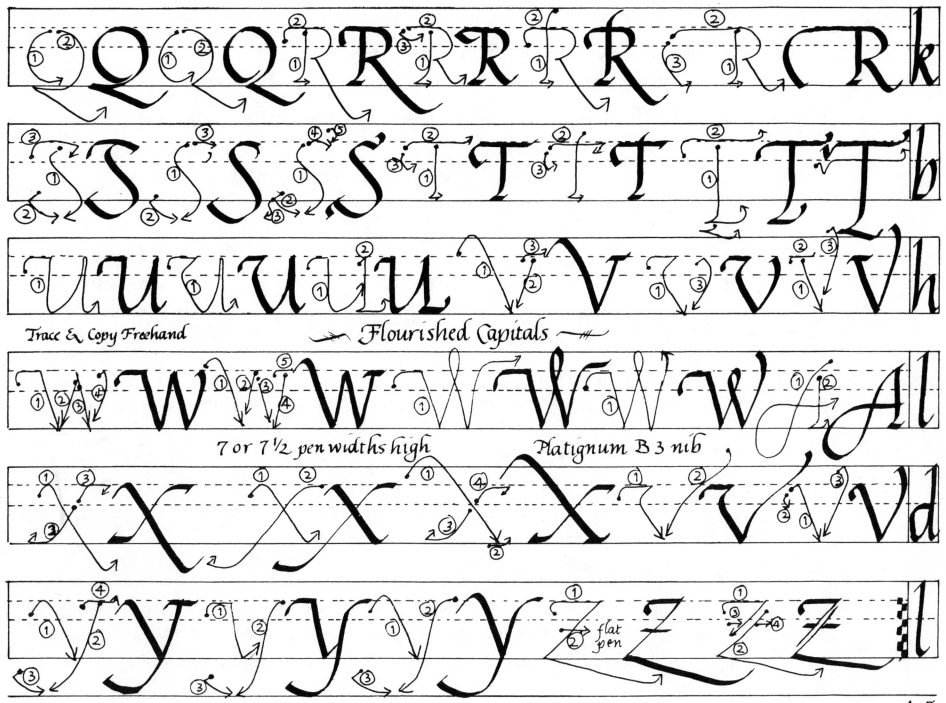

Trace & Copy Freehand     Flourished Capitals

7 or 7½ pen widths high     Platignum B 3 nib

45

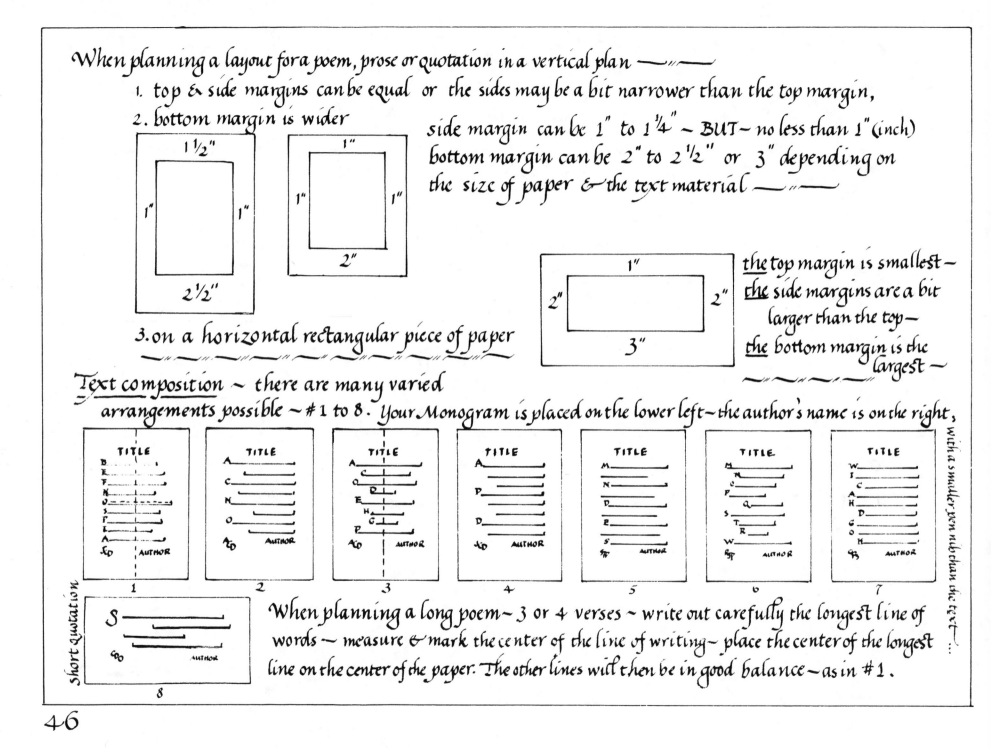

When planning a layout for a poem, prose or quotation in a vertical plan ——
1. top & side margins can be equal or the sides may be a bit narrower than the top margin,
2. bottom margin is wider

side margin can be 1" to 1¼" ~ BUT~ no less than 1" (inch)
bottom margin can be 2" to 2½" or 3" depending on the size of paper & the text material ——

1½"
1"
1"
2½"

1"
1"
1"
2"

1"
2"
2"
3"

the top margin is smallest —
the side margins are a bit larger than the top —
the bottom margin is the largest ~

3. on a horizontal rectangular piece of paper

Text composition ~ there are many varied arrangements possible ~ #1 to 8. Your Monogram is placed on the lower left ~ the author's name is on the right, with a smaller pen nib than the text ~...

1 2 3 4 5 6 7

short quotation

8

When planning a long poem ~ 3 or 4 verses ~ write out carefully the longest line of words ~ measure & mark the center of the line of writing ~ place the center of the longest line on the center of the paper. The other lines will then be in good balance ~ as in #1.

46

# ~ How to Center a Poem ~

1. ~ Place the line guide corresponding to your choice of pen nib under your layout paper.
2. ~ Write out each line of a poem, prose or quotation beginning at the left margin.

> All manner of thing shall be well
> When tongues of flame are in-folded
> Into the crowned knot of fire
> And the fire & the rose are one.
> T. S. Elliot

3. Measure each line of writing with a ruler & mark the centers of each line—.

4. ~ Using the same line guide as in #1 - place it under a piece of tracing paper & draw the lines on the tracing paper.
5. ~ Remove the line guide — now draw a line in the center of the tracing paper~ top to bottom
6. ~ Place the tracing paper center line over the center mark of the first line of the poem~ trace the letters.
7. ~ Repeat #6 on each center mark of each line of the poem.
8. ~ Now the poem is completely centered. If all spelling, spacing, word order is correct the poem can now be

> All manner of thing shall be well
> When tongues of flame are in-folded
> Into the crowned knot of fire
> And the fire & the rose are one.
> T. S. Eliot

transferred to a firm 2 ply Bristol paper (plate finish) by taping the centered poem tracing under the Bristol paper~ then trace the final piece on a light box..

## Steps to Follow in Planning Names to be Written on Certificates

1. Determine which size pen nib can be used for the name —
   — place the B2, Broad or Medium line guides under the certificate —
   — in the area where the name is to be written on the certificate allow for 3 spaces on the line guide

*into the* — *B2*

*lines and* — *Broad*

*spaces on the certificate* — *Medium*

2. Place tracing paper over the line guide being used — trace (in pencil or Flair) the 4 lines used in planning the name (ascender, waist line, base line, descender) — write the name on these lines remember that capitals are lower than ascenders (½ way between waist line & ascender line — ).

3. Find & mark the center of the name —
   — on the wrong side of the certificate — mark the center of the name area

*Anne L. Hoffman*

4. On a light box - place the tracing paper on which the name is written under the certificate in the name area & match the center lines — attach the tracing paper to the certificate — use drafting tape if possible — it is similar to masking tape in appearance but does not not damage paper.

5. Remember to keep a piece of paper under the heel of your hand to protect the paper
   now — trace the name on the certificate —

6. If more than a name is to be written — use the next size nib SMALLER than the name
   — a date is usually done with the Fine nib.

48

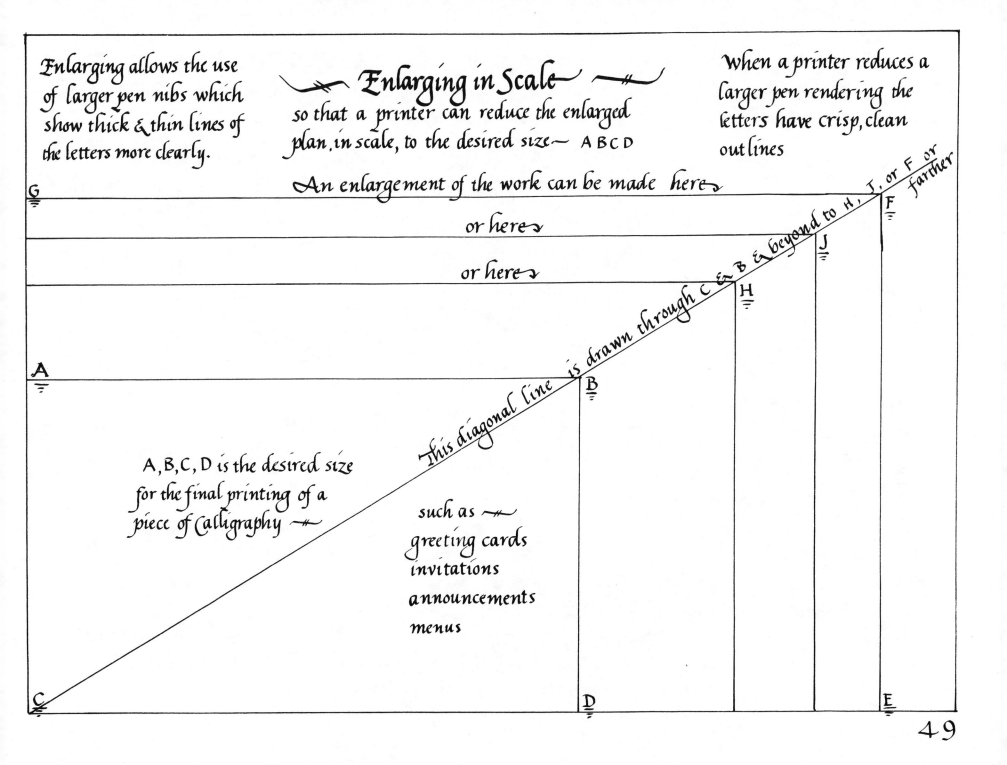

Enlarging allows the use of larger pen nibs which show thick & thin lines of the letters more clearly.

~ Enlarging in Scale ~ *

so that a printer can reduce the enlarged plan, in scale, to the desired size ~ A B C D

When a printer reduces a larger pen rendering the letters have crisp, clean outlines

An enlargement of the work can be made here ~

or here ~

or here ~

This diagonal line is drawn through C & B & beyond to H, J, or F or farther

G

F

J

H

A

B

A, B, C, D is the desired size for the final printing of a piece of Calligraphy ~

such as ~
greeting cards
invitations
announcements
menus

C

D

E

After making a plan for a piece of Calligraphy ~ on tracing paper ~ correcting mistakes in spelling & spacing ~ the tracing paper plan is placed under the final paper ~ the Calligraphy can easily be "trace-copied" directly with the pen using a light box (the tracing paper plan can be seen through a heavier final paper on the light box.)

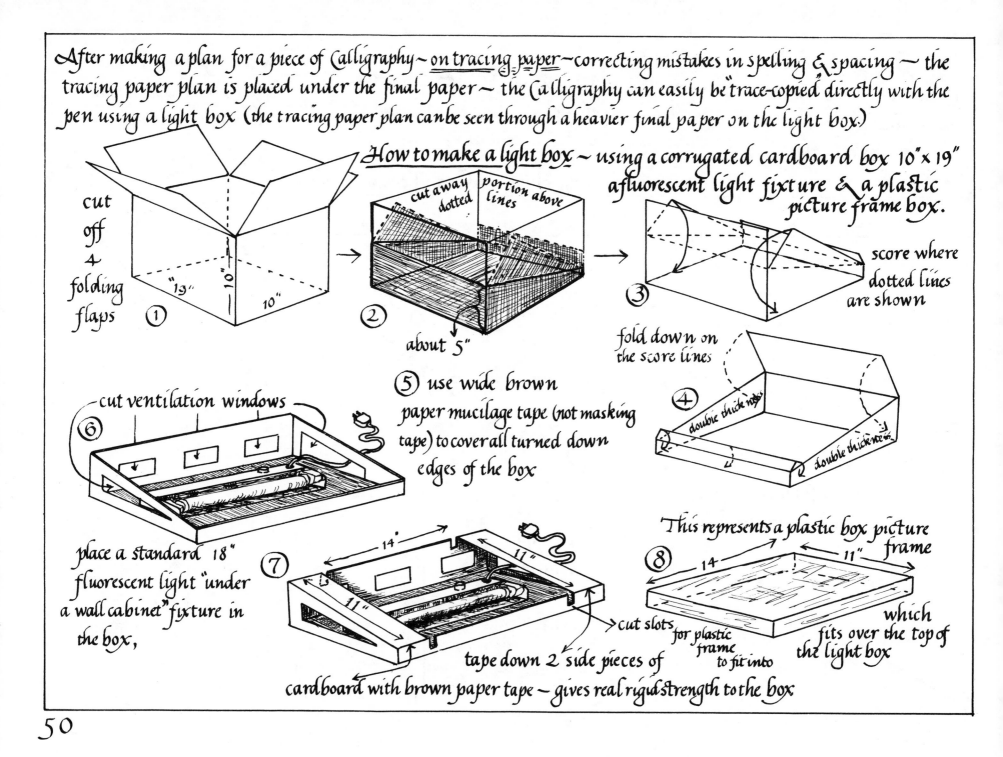

## How to make a light box ~ using a corrugated cardboard box 10" x 19" a fluorescent light fixture & a plastic picture frame box.

cut off 4 folding flaps

① "19"   10"   10"

② cut away dotted portion above lines

about 5"

③ score where dotted lines are shown

④ fold down on the score lines — double thickness — double thickness

⑤ use wide brown paper mucilage tape (not masking tape) to cover all turned down edges of the box

⑥ cut ventilation windows

place a standard 18" fluorescent light "under a wall cabinet" fixture in the box,

⑦ 14"   11"   11"   cut slots for plastic frame to fit into

tape down 2 side pieces of cardboard with brown paper tape ~ gives real rigid strength to the box

⑧ This represents a plastic box picture frame   14   11"   which fits over the top of the light box

# Here is a listing of Calligraphic Societies in the U.S., Canada, England & Holland — a list that grows & changes yearly.

**Association of Berkshire Calligraphers**
c/o Jack Fitterer
RD 1, Rt. 23
Hillsdale, New York 12529

**Calligraphy Guild of Pittsburgh**
P.O. Box 8167
Pittsburgh, Pennsylvania 15217

**Calligraphers Guild**
Box 304
Ashland, Oregon 97520

**Calligraphy Workshop**
14940 Beech Daly Road
Redford, Michigan 48240

**Capitol Calligraphers**
3589 Pringle Road S.E.
Salem, Oregon 97302

**Chautauqua Calligraphers' Guild**
c/o L. Sherman Brooks
Rural Box 321, RFD 2, St. Rt. 380
Jamestown, New York 14701

**Chicago Calligraphy Collective**
P.O. Box 11333
Chicago, Illinois 60611

**Colleagues of Calligraphy**
P.O. Box 4024
St. Paul, Minnesota 55104

**Colorado Calligraphers Guild**
Box 6413
Cherry Creek Station
Denver, Colorado 80206

**Connecticut Calligraphy Society**
P.O. Box 493
New Canaan, Connecticut 06854

**Escribiente**
P.O. Drawer 26718
Albuquerque, New Mexico 87125

**Friends of Calligraphy**
P.O. Box 5194
San Francisco, California 94101

**Handwriters Guild of Toronto**
60 Logandale Road
Willowdale, Ontario CANADA

**Indiana Guild of Calligraphers**
1712 E. 86th Street
Indianapolis, Indiana 46240

**Indiana Calligrapher's Association**
Route 3, Box 192
Floyds Knobs, Indiana 47119

**Indiana Calligrapher's Association**
2501 Pamela Drive
New Albany, Indiana 47150

**Island Scribes**
c/o Janice Glander-Bandyk
1000 East 98th Street
Brooklyn, New York 11236

**Lettering Arts Guild of Boston**
80 Chestnut Street, No. 3
Brookline, Massachusetts 02146

**Mensa's Calligraphy Special Interest Group**
c/o Sally Jackson
2405 Medford Court East
Fort Worth, Texas 76109

**Michigan Association of Calligraphers**
25842 Glover Court
Farmington Hills, Michigan 48018

**New Orleans Calligraphers Association**
6161 Marquette Place
New Orleans, Louisiana 70118

**Opulent Order of Practicing Scribes**
c/o Alice Girand
1310 West 7th Street
Roswell, New Mexico 88201

**Philadelphia Calligrapher's Society**
P.O. Box 7174
Elkins Park, Pennsylvania 19117

**Phoenix Society for Calligraphy**
1709 North 7th Street
Phoenix, Arizona 85006

**Society for Italic Handwriting**
69 Arlington Road
London, N.W. 1 ENGLAND

**Society of Scribes and Illuminators**
c/o Federation of British Craft Societies
43 Earlham Street
London WC2 ENGLAND

**The Fairbank Society**
1970 Fairfield Place
Victoria, BC
V8S 4J4 CANADA

**The Friends for Calligraphy**
1804 Sonoma
Berkeley, California 94707

**The International Association of Master Penmen and Teachers of Handwriting**
2213 Arlington Avenue
Middletown, Ohio 45042

**The League of Hand Binders**
7513 Melrose Avenue
Los Angeles, California 90046

**The Michigan Association of Calligraphers**
c/o Susanne Ebel
25842 Glover Court
Farmington, Michigan 48018

**The New Haven Calligraphers Guild**
c/o Jay C. Rochelle
27 High Street
New Haven, Connecticut 06510

**Tidewater Calligraphy Guild**
c/o Michael R. Sull
220 Cortland Lane
Virginia Beach, Virginia 23452

**Goose Quill Guild**
c/o Allen Q. Wong
Department of Art
Oregon State University
Corvallis, Oregon 97331

**Society of Scribes**
P.O. Box 933
New York, NY 10022

**Society for Calligraphy**
P.O. Box 64174
Los Angeles, California 90064

**Society for Calligraphy and Handwriting**
c/o The Factory of Visual Art
4649 Sunnyside North
Seattle, Washington 98103

**Society for Italic Handwriting**
British Columbia Branch
P.O. Box 48390
Bentall Centre
Vancouver, British Columbia
V7X 1A2 CANADA

**San Antonio Calligrapher's Guild**
2407 Shadow Cliff
San Antonio, Texas 78232

**Valley Calligraphy Guild**
3241 Kevington
Eugene, Oregon 97405

**Vereniging Mercator**
Gaasterlandstraat 96
Haarlem, HOLLAND

**Washington Calligrapher's Guild**
Box 23818
Washington, DC 20024

**Western American Branch of the Society for Italic Handwriting**
c/o Mrs. Jo Ann DiSciullo
6800 S.E. 32nd Avenue
Portland, Oregon 97202

**Write On Calligraphers**
No. 5, 7929 196th S.W.
Edmonds, Washington 98020

## This list was printed in the Calligraphy Quarterly published by the N.Y. Soc. of Scribes.

*Suppliers*
David Green
176 W.Jaxine Dr.
Altadena, CA 91001
(Reed pens with reservoir, felt pens, many sizes.
Write for brochure and price list.)

The H Co.
1133 Broadway
New York, NY
(Big H marker and Midi Marker. Large felt tip
markers.)

M. Schwartz & Son, Inc.
321-325 E.3rd St.,
New York, NY 10007
(Feathers for quills.)

H.Brand & Co.,Ltd.
Brent Way - High Street,
Brentford, Middlesex, England,
TW8 8ET.
(Vellums)

L. Cornellissen & Son
22 Great Queen Street,
London, WC2, England
(Dry pigment colours, gums and resins.)

Cando Hoshino
1541 Clement St.,
San Francisco, CA 94118
(Japanese stick colour, pigments, brushes, papers.)

George M. Whiley, Ltd.
Firth Rd., Houstoun Industrial Estate
Livingston, West Lothian EH54 5DJ,
Scotland.
(Gold suppliers - no overseas orders under
100 English pounds.)

Coit Calligraphers, Inc.
P.O.Box 1206
Fairfield, CT 06430
(9 varieties of pen nibs from 1/14" to 1" wide.)

Fine Art Materials, Inc.
530 La Guardia Pl.
New York, NY

McManus & Morgan
2506 W. 7th St.
Los Angeles, CA
(Paper supplies.)

*This list was printed in a Newsletter of the British Soc. of Scribes & Illuminators.*

Joseph Torch
29 W.15th St.
New York 10011
(Extensive supplies and handmade paper.)

Chinatown Book Store
70a Mott St.
New York, NY 10013

Hong Kong Book Store
72 Mott St.
New York, NY 10013
(Both Chinatown and Hong Kong Book Stores
stock covered ink stones of nice dimensions
for about $5.00 - no mail delivery.)

Chew Chong Tai & Co.
905 Grant Ave.
San Francisco, CA 94126
(Ink stone and ink stick.)

Callics Calligraphy Supply
P.O.Box 1787
Monterey, CA 93940
(408-372-9210)
(Homemade papers, gilding materials and vellum)

Twinrocker Handmade Paper
Brookston, IN.

The Scriptorium Benedictine
410 S.Michigan Blvd
Chicago, IL 60605
(Write for catalogue/price list.)

Saylor's Art Supplies
420 E. 4th St.,
Long Beach, CA
(General art supplies and some calligraphic
supplies.)

New York Central Supply Co.
62 3rd Ave.
New York, NY 10003
(Extensive calligraphy catalogue for mail order or
showroom.)

Andrews/Nelson/Whitehead
7 Laight St.
New York NY10013
(Paper supplies.)

Falkiner Fine Papers
4 Mart St.
London, WC2, England.
(Pens, quills, brushes, ink, illuminating supplies,
pigment, paper, etc. Write for catalogue/price list.)

Pentalic Corp.
132 W.22nd St.
New York 10011
(Calligraphy and illuminating materials as well as
books dealing with the lettering arts. Write for
catalogue.)

Special Papers
Rt. No 2
West Redding, CT 06896

Art Media
820 SW 10th Ave.
Portland, Oregon 97205

*Publications*
Italix
Haywood House
P.O.Box 279
Fair Lawn, NJ 07410
(Published quarterly $10.00/year.)

Italimuse
Fred Eager
3128 Burr St.
Fairfield, CT 06430
(Published yearly, $2.00 for 1976.
Write to be on mailing list - supplies available.)

Calligrafree - Newsletter & Supplies
43 Ankara Ave.        catalog available
Brookville, OH 45309.

*Publishers*
Museum Books Inc.
48 E. 43rd St., New York, NY 10017
(Hard to get calligraphy and graphic art books.
Will order on request - no catalogues.)

David R. Godine, Publisher
306 Dartmouth St., Boston, MA 02116
(Brochure on the Godine line of books on typo-
graphy and calligraphy - good discounts.)

| Books about Calligraphy & Related Subjects — also sources | |
|---|---|
| Calligraphy Today ~ Heather Child  Pentalic, N.Y. | The History & Technique of Lettering ~ Alexander Nesbitt  Dover, N.Y. |
| An ABC Book ~ Eric Lindegren  Pentalic, N.Y. | Three Classics of Italian Calligraphy, Arrighi, Tagliente, & Palatino — Dover, N.Y. |
| The Young Letterer ~ Tony Hart  Fred Warne & Co., Inc., N.Y. | Celtic & Anglo Saxon Painting  Carl Nordenfalk ~ Geo. Braziller, N.Y. |
| Two Thousand Years of Calligraphy ~ P.W. Philby ~ Taplinger Publ. Co., N.Y. | Recollections of the Lyceum & Chautauqua Circuits ~ R.F. DaBoll ~ Bond Wheelwright Publ. Co., Freeport, Maine |
| Calligraphy, The Golden Age & Its Revival  Schultz ~ Riddle | Manuscript and Inscription Letters ~ Edward Johnston & Eric Gill — Pentalic, N.Y. |
| Edward Johnston ~ Priscilla Johnston  Taplinger Publ. Co., N.Y. | Writing, Illuminating & Lettering ~ Edward Johnston ~ Pentalic, N.Y. |
| The Art of Written Forms ~ Donald Anderson  Holt, Rinehart & Winston, N.Y. | Formal Penmanship & Other Papers ~ Edward Johnston, Edited by Heather Child ~ Lund Humphries Publ. Ltd., London |
| The 26 Letters ~ Oscar Ogg  Thomas Crowell Co., N.Y. | Lettering ~ Graily Hewitt  Pentalic Corp., N.Y. |
| The Craftsman's Handbook ~ Cennino Cennini  Dover, N.Y. | The Calligrapher's Handbook  Pentalic Corp., N.Y. |
| Decorative Alphabets & Initials ~ Alexander Nesbitt ~ Dover, N.Y. | The Art of Lettering With the Broad Pen ~ Byron MacDonald  Pentalic Corp., N.Y. |
| Celtic Art, The Methods of Construction ~ George Bain, ~ Dover, N.Y. | Written Letters ~ Jacqueline Svaren ~ Bond Wheelwright Publ. Co., ~ Freeport, Maine |
| The Book of Kells ~ Alfred A. Knopf ~ N.Y. | Pen Lettering ~ Ann Camp ~ Dryad Press, Leicester, England |
| The Art of Fine Lettering ~ Michaeline Lesiak  Univ. of Notre Dame Press, Notre Dame, Indiana | Calligraphic Lettering ~ Ralph Douglas  Watson ~ Guptill Publications |

## Books about Calligraphy & Related Subjects — also sources

| | |
|---|---|
| Italic Calligraphy & Handwriting ~ Lloyd J. Reynolds <br> Pentalic Corp., ~ N.Y. | Treasury of Alphabets & Lettering ~ Jan Tschichold ~ <br> Reinhold Publishers |
| The Italic Way to Beautiful Handwriting ~ Fred Eager <br> Collier Books, MacMillan Publ. Co., ~ N.Y. | A Treasury of Design for Artists & Craftsmen ~ <br> Gregory Mirow ~ Dover, ~ N.Y. |
| The Art of Hand Lettering ~ Helm Wotzkow <br> Dover Publications, Inc., ~ N.Y. | Manuscript Painting at the Court of France ~ 14th Century <br> Francois Avril ~ George Braziller ~ N.Y. |
| Elements of Lettering ~ John Howard Benson & Arthur <br> Graham Carey ~ McGraw Hill, ~ N.Y. | The Lindisfarne Gospels ~ Janet Backhouse <br> Cornell University Press, Ithaca, N.Y. |
| Lettering ~ Hermann Degering ~ <br> Pentalic Corp., N.Y. | Lettering & Drawing, The Moving Line ~ <br> Nicolette Gray ~ Oxford University Press, London |
| Irene Wellington Omnibus Copybook ~ <br> Pentalic Corp., ~ N.Y. | The Craft of Lettering ~ John R. Biggs <br> Pitman Publishing Corp. ~ N.Y. |
| A Book of Sample Scripts ~ Edward Johnston ~ <br> H M S O ~ London | Speedball Textbook of Pen & Brush Lettering <br> Hunt Manufacturing Co. |
| Modern Scribes & Lettering Artists <br> Taplinger Publishing Co., ~ N.Y. | A Dictionary For Calligraphers ~ Robert C. Hyde <br> Martin Press ~ Los Angeles |
| An Illustrated History of Writing ~ Jan Tschichold, <br> Zwemmer ~ | Medieval Calligraphy, Its History & Technique ~ <br> Marc Drogin ~ Allenheld & Schramm, Montclair, N.J. |
| Woman's Day Book of Calligraphy ~ Dennis Droge <br> & Janice Glander Blandyk ~ Simon & Schuster, N.Y. | The Story of Writing ~ Donald Jackson ~ <br> Taplinger Publishing Co., N.Y. |
| Lettering: The History & Technique ~ <br> Alexander Nesbitt ~ Prentice Hall, ~ N.Y. | The Belles Heures of Jean, Duke de Berry ~ <br> George Braziller ~ N.Y. |
| The Alphabet Source Book ~ Oscar Ogg ~ <br> Dover, N.Y. | Celtic Illuminative Art in the Gospel Books of <br> Durrow, Lindisfarne & Kells ~ |
| Historic Alphabets & Initials ~ Carol Belanger Grafton <br> Dover ~ N.Y. | S.F.H. Robinson ~ Hodges, Figgis & Co. Ltd., Dublin, Ire. |

ascenders

capitals

waist line

base line

descenders

base line

base line

base line

Letter height ~ 5 pen widths ~ Platignum B-4 nib ~ Calligraphic formal mode ~ Guide sheet #1

55

base line

base line

base line

base line

base line

base line

Letter height ~ 5 pen widths ~ Platignum B3 nib ~ Calligraphic formal mode ~ Guide sheet #2

57

letter height ~ 5 pen widths ~ Platignum B-2 nib    Calligraphic formal mode ~ guide sheet # 3

59

*Letter height ~ 5 pen widths ~ Platignum Broad or B nib ~ Calligraphic formal mode*        *Line Guide sheet # 4*

*Letter height ~ 5 pen widths ~ Platignum Medium nib ~ Calligraphic formal mode*     *Line Guide sheet #5*

63

Letter height ~ 5 pen widths ~ Platignum Fine nib ~ Calligraphic formal mode ~      Line guide sheet # 6

65

Body of letter height ~ 5 pen widths ~ Platignum B-4 nib ~ Calligraphic formal mode

Body of letter height~ 5 pen widths~Platignum B~3 nib~ Calligraphic formal mode

Body of letter height~5 pen widths~Platignum B-2 nib~Calligraphic formal mode

Body of letter height ~ 5 pen widths ~ Platignum Broad nib ~ Calligraphic formal mode

Body of letter height ~ 5 pen widths ~ Platignum Medium nib ~ Calligraphic formal mode

Body of letter height ~ 5 pen widths ~ Platignum Fine nib ~ Calligraphic Formal Mode

Christmas comes to us again All errors to dissolve. The promise which transcends all else is destined to evolve...

As each year comes to its end Progress may seem dimmer still. For this world there'd be little hope~ But for Christmas inspired goodwill...

Each of us can build new hope, Transforming human ills. God's promise, which is the ultimate plan, Renews~restores~fulfills

Confidence in eternal life & life's treasures unprofaned

are God's gift to each of us. For all it is ordained...

Joy to you

A Christmas Card that folds four points to the center. No envelope needed.

Christmas again, Thoughts turn to the Babe,

Christmas again, Love's message remade.

Christmas again, Children's hearts are alight,

Christmas again, For that magical night.

Christmas again, Hope springs anew,

Christmas again, God's great gift to you....

Christmas card using 5 pointed music dip pen

The Shadows

All hushed the trees are waiting
      On tiptoe for the sight
Of moonrise shedding splendor
      Across the dusk of night.
Ah, now the moon is risen,
      And lo, without a sound
The trees all write their welcome
      Far along the ground.

B.B.

For yesterday
is but a dream
and tomorrow
is only a vision
but today
well lived
makes yesterday
a dream of happiness
and every tomorrow
a vision of hope

Italic renditions
by beginning students

M.M.

81

If a man does not keep pace
with his companions,
perhaps it is because
he hears
a different drummer.

Let him step to
the music which he hears,
however measured
or far away.

Henry David Thoreau

## Days

Some days my thoughts are just cocoons —
all cold, & dull, & blind,
They hang from dripping branches
in the grey woods of my mind;
And other days they drift & shine —
such free & flying things —
I find the gold-dust in my hair,
left by their brushing wings.

— Karle Wilson Baker

Italic renditions
by beginning students

There are five pages ~ beginning with a white cover paper & "flyleaf" ~ following the canon diagram on the next page (84) ~ which are to be removed from this book. These four pages & the cover page are to be folded in half & sewn together by hand to make a single section (or single signature) book.

When making one's own book the writing is done before sewing the book pages together...

"The Canon" ~ or book page form is planned to give an opened book a balanced appearance ~ ....

The double page text areas can be made for any size book ~ large or small ~ by following the numbered lines as shown on the next page. ~ The result will be margins & text areas that are correctly & historically proportioned ~.

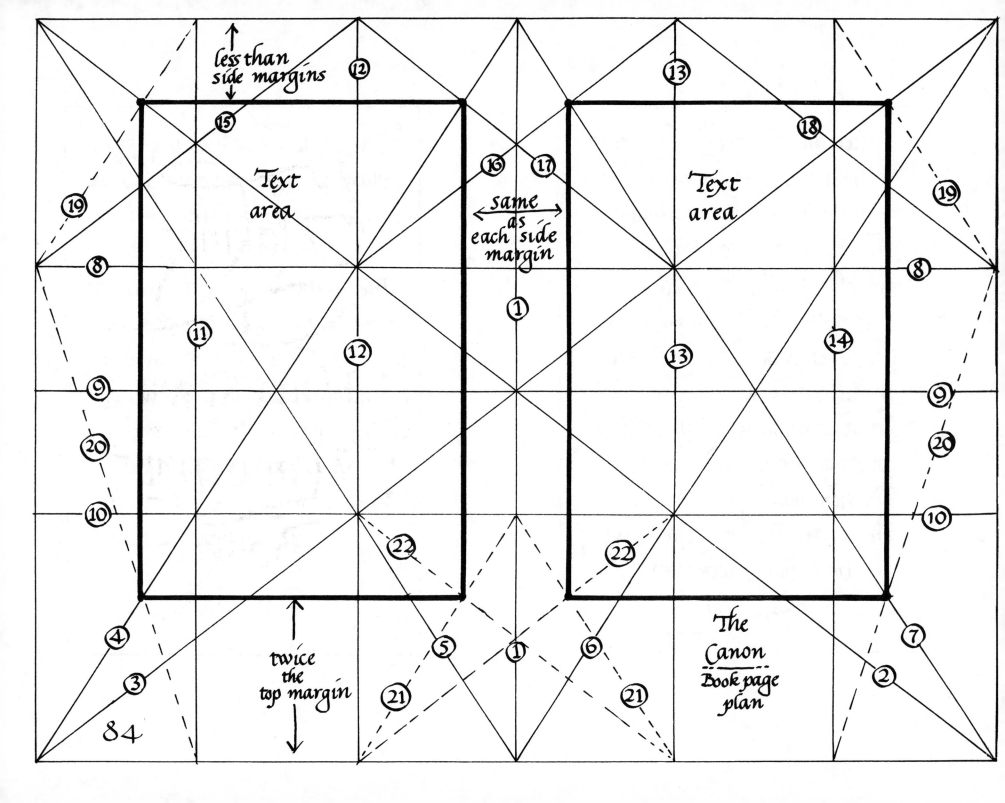

less than
side margins

⑫

⑬

⑮

⑱

⑯ ⑰

Text
area

Text
area

⑲

⑲

same
as
each side
margin

⑧

⑧

①

⑪

⑭

⑫

⑬

⑨

⑨

⑳

⑳

⑩

⑩

㉒

㉒

④

⑦

⑤

①

⑥

The
Canon
Book page
plan

③

⑤

①

⑥

②

twice
the
top margin

㉑

㉑

84

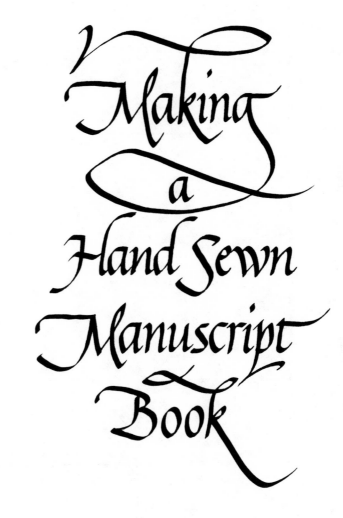

Making
a
Hand Sewn
Manuscript
Book

flyleaf

flyleaf

(Opening Page)

A Manuscript Book

( Colophon )

Calligraphy by
Muriel M. Parker
——//—//—//—//—

7.

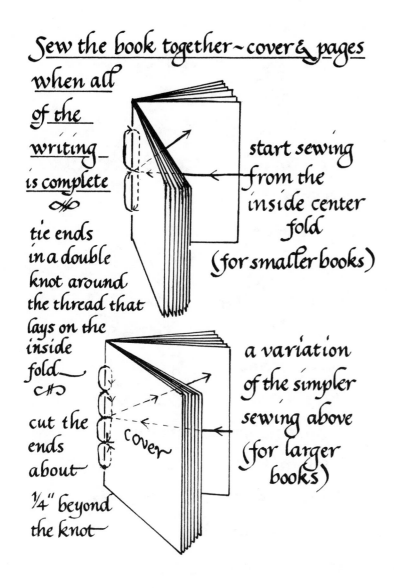

Sew the book together~cover & pages

when all
of the
writing
is complete
∞

tie ends
in a double
knot around
the thread that
lays on the
inside
fold
∞

cut the
ends
about

¼" beyond
the knot

cover

start sewing
from the
inside center
fold
(for smaller books)

a variation
of the simpler
sewing above
(for larger
books)

6.

Title Page

Making
a
Manuscript Book

An illustration
can be drawn here.

## Subjects for Manuscript
### ~ books ~

Ballads & folk songs

Baptismal Service ~ Birth, baby
book

Marriage Service

Alphabet exemplars ~ ABCdarium

Family tree & Register

Local History     Church events

Epitaphs     Friendship

Recipe book     Gratitude

Guest book     Birthday

Favorite poems ~ original poems

Photo albums     Graduation

Anniversary     Welcome

Favorite maxims

Farewell presentation

Margins in books
The combined center margins &
the 2 outside vertical margins are
all the same width.
                    The top margin
is less than the three vertical margins.
The bottom margin is usually <u>two</u>
times the width of the top one.
                         The
"golden Triangle" automatically
measures the above described margins.

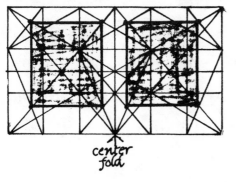

center
fold

4.

A Manuscript Book
Planning & writing a single section (single signature) book is a basic
exercise for the beginning Calligraphy
student.
          Size of the page
          Usually the size of the manu-
script book page is determined by the
size of the paper being used & the way
that paper can be folded.

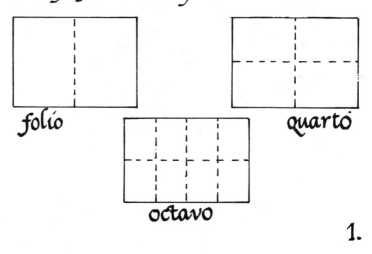

folio

quarto

octavo

1.

The make-up of the book

It is not possible for a beginning project to complete more than a simple single section book. It will be sewn with linen or cotton thread into a stiff card stock paper cover.

A dummy book is first made, then pages are numbered beginning at the first text page. The figure below, is the plan for the pages of a book.

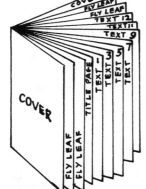

Decide the number of words for a page & then plan the number of pages needed for writing the content of the book. It is better to have too many pages than not enough. An extra fly leaf at the end of the book is acceptable.

Make a line guide on a piece of tracing paper using the "Golden Triangle" method of establishing traditional page format. (the Canon).

The first text page is on the right side (recto) of the book. The title page is also on the right side, & is designed when the text is completed.

# A Practical Handbook for Practicing

## The

# Informal Cursive Mode

## of

# Italic Writing

Muriel M. Parker

95

# Introduction

There are <u>two</u> Major Differences between the Calligraphic formal mode & the Cursive informal mode of Italic writing. The <u>First</u> is ~ the "pen width-height" of the body of the letters.

←ascender
g ←body height
←descender

The Calligraphic formal mode is ~ 5 pen widths ⟋ a

The Cursive informal mode is ~ 4 pen widths ⟋ a    (sometimes 3 or 3½) pen widths high

The <u>Second</u> is ~ formal letters are separate within words ~ (ex) magnanimity

whereas informal letters have joins connecting some of them ~ (ex) magnanimity

In this second section ~ Informal trace & copy pages are planned to familiarize the student with the joins, also called ligatures or ties, between letters in words. Not all of the letters are joined, making an easy flow of writing by providing lift points.

## ~ Types of Joins ~

diagonal joins <u>into</u> & <u>out of</u> the letters ~ a d c e v m n w ~~~        Two letters never joined ~ b & z.

diagonal joins <u>only into</u> the letters ~ g j o p q r s t v w x y

horizontal joins <u>into</u> & <u>out of</u> the letters ~ o f t (ex.) foot often

three letters ~ <u>ascenders</u> ~ are <u>not</u> joined to a <u>preceding letter</u> ~ h k l ~ but join diagonally <u>out</u> of each

five letters ~ <u>descenders</u> ~ are <u>not</u> joined to a <u>following letter</u> ~ g j pq & y

An <u>Ultrafine</u> Flair pen is used to practice the smaller Italic shapes in the simple line letter forms before writing on the trace & copy pages that are done with the Medium & Fine nibs.

When <u>writing a letter</u> after learning the joins it is advisable to use <u>line guides</u> under correspondence paper. Broad, Medium & Fine nib <u>line guides</u> are provided at the back of this section. There is also a line guide for addressing an envelope ~ . . . . .

96

Platignum Broad pen ~ Cursive Mode ~ 4 pen widths high

a c d e i m n u ~ _diagonal joins into & out of letters_

g j o p r s t v w x y ~ _diagonal joins into - not out of letters_

h l k ~ _diagonal joins only out of the letters_

fo or to ~ _horizontal joins out of_ f, o & t

b & z ~ _stand free - no joins in or out_

double letters ~   a<u>tt</u>ain  ga<u>ss</u>es  a<u>ff</u>air  o<u>o</u>ze  lo<u>tt</u>o  ta<u>ll</u>  o<u>ff</u>

~ Join Practice ~

Trace
an na as say at ta aim man du add en ep ed es ewe ea

copy

Trace
cup cent camel code cocoa door down dove dozen able

copy

97

dip day den dun cling deep deed fu fa fo fi fen fan fox

funny foggy hu ku hi ki hear keep lip him limit lo

mo mi me mu many ni ny nm np ns nt nx neice num

oa oo op oq or os ov ox oy oe oi out put puppy pony pat

tu te to ti ta tc ts tr ft fj under our four tower tonal

upon utterly vase aviator win trowel zen adze usual

Informal Cursive Mode      ~ ~ ~ Joins Practice ~ ~ ~      Platignum Broad Nib ~ 4 pen widths

Informal Calligraphy trace & copy exercise ~ Platignum Broad nib

Trace Line Italic cursive handwriting began in Italy in the 15th

Copy Line

century & was used by Vatican Scribes for writing the many

Papal briefs. It spread over all of Christendom & was widely

used by scribes on the European continent & the British Isles.

It was in 1522 that the first writing manual was printed ~

composed by Ludovico degli Arrighi, a writing master at the

Informal Cursive Mode ~ for letter writing ~ uses joins (ligatures) ~ 4 pen widths high letter body

Vatican. Other manuals soon followed, by Antonio Tagliente in

1524 & Giambattista Palatino in 1544. After the Thirty

years War, in 1648, the pointed pen eventually replaced

the square cut nib & Italic, with the sensitive thick & thin line,

gradually went out of style. ~~~ A revival of Italic writing has

been in progress, beginning with a little book on Chancery Cur-

sive handwriting written by Mrs. Robert Bridges in England at

Informal Cursive Mode ~ for letter writing ~ uses ligatures (joins) ~ 4 pen widths body of letter height

the turn of the 20th Century. As a result of enthusiastic efforts

of such men as Edward Johnston & Alfred Fairbank in the early

years of this century, the Italic way has become a popular

movement here & abroad among many people who are desir-

ous of an improvement in the scribble & illegible writing so

prevalent today. ("La Operina" is the title of Arrighi's manual.)

Informal Cursive Mode ~ for letter writing ~ 4 pen widths high

Italic Letters review practise ~ for Cursive writing with the Platignum Medium Pen nib

TRACE writing with the medium pen is easier to learn if words with ligatures (joins)

COPY

TRACE are first practised with an Ultra Fine Flair felt pen or a sharp pencil. Often

COPY

TRACE when the writing becomes smaller ~ medium & fine nibs ~ there is some

COPY

TRACE difficulty at first to maintain a particular letter in the true Italic shape ~

COPY

TRACE such as a b c d e f g h i j k l m n o p q r s t u v w x y z Aa Bb Cc Dd Ee Ff Gg

COPY

TRACE Hh Ii Jj Kk Ll Mm Nn Oo Pp Qq Rr Ss Tt Uu Vv Vv Ww

COPY

TRACE Xx Yy Zz // Unless a man under takes more than he possibly can do

COPY

TRACE A H J M N // he will never do all he can do. ~ Henry Drummond

COPY

In the first writing book of Italic handwriting, printed in 1522, & written by

Ludovico degli Arrighi, rules for each letter are given in a charming manner...

"So, my Reader, you must know that of the small letters of the Alphabet, some may

be tied with those that follow, some may not. Those that may be tied with followers

are here written, namely, a c d f i k l m n s t u, of which a d i k l m n u are tied

with any that follow: But c f s t tie only with some: The rest of the Alphabet, to wit,

be g h o p q r x y z ought not to be tied to the following letter. But to tie or not to

tie, I leave to your judgment provided that the letters be equal.

Cursive mode ~ Platignum Medium nib ~ 4 pen widths letter body height ~ for writing letters ~ informal mode

103

This is a practice page in the cursive mode, using an Ultra fine flair felt pen, to review the

Italic letters discipline before writing with the Platignum Fine pen nib. Writing habits acquired in

earlier years sometimes surface, & steady concentration while writing Italic with a very small

pen is necessary. Correspondence may seem laborious at first. Time, determination & practice

will make writing in Italic become a reality. Here are 2 suggestions for composing a letter —

1. Write short letters. Think out, before writing, the most brief wording to express your thoughts

2. Write out in one's original handwriting all that one wishes to include in a letter — then copy

it over in Italic. (excellent practice)

Friends, relatives, business people, & even the postman, when sent a letter & an envelope addressed

in Italic, all feel that someone cared enough to send their very best.

Arrighi's Operina

The First Writing Book ~ 1522

for learning to write the Chancery letters

Anyone who wishes to learn to write the cursive or Chancery letter ought to observe the follow-

ing forms &, first he should learn to make these 2 strokes, to wit —/, with one of which begin

all the Chancery letters. Of these two strokes the one is flat & thick, the other is slanting & thin

as you can see here noted —/—/—/—/. Do first the flat & thick stroke, that is — — — with which,

reversed &, turning upon itself, one commences; thus one begins the following letters — — — — — —

a b c d f g h k l o g s x. The rest of the Alphabet begins with the second stroke, slanting & thin,

ascending with the edge of the pen & then returning downward in this way — — i e p t u j z y o ~ .

With apologies to Mr. Arrighi — m n r v & w are not now "slanting & thin thusly m n p r v w.

Today we write these letters beginning with a narrow turn  ⁊⁊ — m n p r v w ("p" is turned ~ not pointed)

Informal Cursive mode ~ 4 pen widths letter body height ~ Platignum Fine pen nib ~ Quote from pp. 4 & 5 "Operina"

105

113 Lexington Rd.
Bel Air Maryland 21014
14 November 1975

Dear Muriel,
As our Calligraphy classes come to an end, I wanted to tell you that I have sincerely enjoyed learning Italic writing and find it interesting and challenging.

Hours have become minutes during the time that I have spent in class and practice sessions. I am very proud to have had the opportunity to study Italic writing under your guidance & also equally proud of my progress & accomplishments.
Sincerely
Fay Sigler

---

March 5, 1979

Dear Muriel,
I said I wasn't going to become one of those "fanatics" who write their letters in Italic, so, of course, here I am ... I got inspired by those letters you showed me from A. Lincoln. The more I practice, the easier it gets. I've written three eight-to-twelve-page letters in the last two days!

I never thought I'd ever be writing in Italic with such speed! Your time-table of two years or so was quite accurate.

Nothing else new to report. Keep healthy!

Love,
Pat

---

R. Mark Mitchell
218 E. Preston St.
Baltimore, Md.
21202

10
Robert Frost
AMERICAN POET

Mrs. Edward H. Parker
6905 Moyer Ave.
Baltimore, Md.
21234

---

June 1, 1974

Dear Mrs. Parker,
How pleased I was to receive your package!! Thank-you very much. The equipment arrived in the nick of time. It was very kind of you to give me your cyclgraf rulers along with the charts.

I have just calculated 3 more charts and again Biorhythm came through.

who had had a terri- in December. A criti- with the accident! be a convert. She en's book for next odern Myths and u can give a lecture

Affectionately,
Mark

---

April 1, 1979

Dear Judy —
Many happy returns of your Big Day on the ninth. I'm sorry we're not celebrating with you.
We got the bad news about Ben Nevis via the golf course Saturday afternoon. It must have been a rough race! Did you wear the silk undershirt? I can't wait to hear every detail.
Charlie and Basil arrived home from Golf School ten minutes ago — Would you believe that they're now sitting in front of the T.V. watching the Sunday golf?!'B. complained that his ears were exhausted from peeling!
Glad you weren't on the road to see me having a ball on F.T. Gieske's Go-Cart this week. They're great fun and not too noisy.
I found your glasses and Cornelia's mug — all safe. Since this is my calligraphy homework "2 birds - etc." must stop at the proper place. Have a marvelous time.

you —
Kitty

---

Each of these letters done in the Informal Cursive Mode illustrates the individuality of each person.

---

CWagner - Owings Mills, Md. 21117 - U.S.A.

Air Mail

Mrs. Alexander H. Russell
Connaught Hotel
Carlos Place
London - W1Y - 6AL
England ~

Platignum Broad Nib Line Guide ~ Informal Cursive Mode ~ $\frac{4}{=}$ pen widths for body height of letters

Platignum Medium Pen nib line guide ~ Cursive mode ~ 4 pen widths letter body height ~ for writing letters

109

*Informal Cursive mode line guide ~ Platignum Fine nib ~ 4 pen width - body height of letters ~ for correspondence letters*

111

| A | C | E | F | N | O | R | S | T | U | V | W | X | Z | B | H | L |
|---|---|---|---|---|---|---|---|---|---|---|---|---|---|---|---|---|
| a | c: | e: | m | n | o: | r: | s | t | u | v | w | x | z | b | h | l |

A B C E F H I J K L N O P R S T U V Y Z G

a b c d e f g h h j k l m o p q r s t u v

115

Cursive mode ~ Platignum Fine nib - 4 pen widths body of letter ht. ~ for writing letters

return address

Addressee – 4 pen widths

Envelope addressing line guide

Medium pen nib

return address – 3½ pen widths

place either line guide inside an envelope

return address – 3½ pen widths

Fine pen nib

Envelope addressing guide lines

Addressee – 4 pen widths

return address

'This workbook has evolved over seven
years of teaching Italic Calligraphy
at home, in a craft shop, at Harford
Community College, Bel Air, Maryland,
Essex Community College, Essex, Maryland,
& at Roland Park Country School,
Baltimore, Maryland.